Ideas & Daily Life
in the
Muslim World Today

Abdul Hakeem Tamer

MASON CREST
PHILADELPHIA

Mason Crest
450 Parkway Drive, Suite D
Broomall, PA 19008
www.masoncrest.com

©2017 by Mason Crest, an imprint of National Highlights, Inc.

All rights reserved. No part of this publication may be reproduced or transmitted in any form or by any means, electronic or mechanical, including photocopying, recording, taping, or any information storage and retrieval system, without permission from the publisher.

Printed and bound in the United States of America.

CPSIA Compliance Information: Batch #UI2016.
For further information, contact Mason Crest at 1-866-MCP-Book.

First printing
1 3 5 7 9 8 6 4 2

Library of Congress Cataloging-in-Publication Data

on file at the Library of Congress
ISBN: 978-1-4222-3671-0 (hc)
ISBN: 978-1-4222-8109-3 (ebook)

Understanding Islam series ISBN: 978-1-4222-3670-3

Table of Contents

INTRODUCTION 5
    Dr. Camille Pecastaing, Ph.D.
1. POLLING THE ISLAMIC WORLD 9
2. THE ROOTS OF THE MODERN ISLAMIC WORLD 15
3. WHAT IT MEANS TO BE A MUSLIM TODAY.................29
4. VIEWS ON CULTURE AND VALUES 43
5. WOMEN AND ISLAM 61
6. VIEWS ON CONFLICTS IN PALESTINE AND SYRIA 71
7. MUSLIM VIEWS ON OTHER ISSUES..........................87
CHRONOLOGY 100
SERIES GLOSSARY 104
FURTHER READING 105
INTERNET RESOURCES 106
INDEX 107
CONTRIBUTORS 112

KEY ICONS TO LOOK FOR:

Words to Understand: These words with their easy-to-understand definitions will increase the reader's understanding of the text, while building vocabulary skills.

Sidebars: This boxed material within the main text allows readers to build knowledge, gain insights, explore possibilities, and broaden their perspectives by weaving together additional information to provide realistic and holistic perspectives.

Research Projects: Readers are pointed toward areas of further inquiry connected to each chapter. Suggestions are provided for projects that encourage deeper research and analysis.

Text-Dependent Questions: These questions send the reader back to the text for more careful attention to the evidence presented there.

Series Glossary of Key Terms: This back-of-the book glossary contains terminology used throughout this series. Words found here increase the reader's ability to read and comprehend higher-level books and articles in this field.

Islam: Core Beliefs and Practices
Ideas & Daily Life in the Muslim World Today
Islamism & Fundamentalism in the Modern World
The Monotheistic Faiths: Judaism, Christianity, and Islam
Muslim Heroes and Holy Places
Muslims in America
An Overview: Who are the Muslims?
The Struggle for Identity: Islam and the West

Introduction

by Camille Pecastaing, Ph.D.

Islam needs no introduction. Everyone around the world old enough is likely to have a formed opinion of Islam and Muslims. The cause of this wide recognition is, sadly, the recurrent eruptions of violence that have marred the recent—and not so recent—history of the Muslim world. A violence that has also selectively followed Muslim immigrants to foreign lands, and placed Islam at the front and center of global issues.

Notoriety is why Islam needs no simple introduction, but far more than that. Islam needs a correction, an exposition, a full discussion of its origins, its principles, its history, and of course of what it means to the 1.5 to 2 billion contemporaries associated with it, whether by origins, tradition, practice or belief.

The challenge is that Islam has a long history, spread over fourteen centuries. Its principles have been contested from the beginning, the religion has known schism after schism, and politico-theological issues instructed all sorts of violent conflict. The history of Islam is epic, leaving Islam today as a mosaic of diverse sects and practices: Sunnism, Shi'ism, Sufism, Salafism, Wahhabism, and of course, Jihadism. The familiarity of those terms often masks ignorance of the distinctions between them.

Islam is many things to many people, and while violent radicals occupy the headlines, what a Muslim is in the 21st century is practically indefinable. Islam is present on every continent; the religion of billionaires and of the poorest people in the world, the religion of kings and revolutionaries, of illiterate pastoralists and nuclear scientists, of fundamentalist theologians and avant-garde artists. Arabic is the language of Islam, the language of the Qur'an, but most Muslims only speak other tongues. Many Muslims indulge in moderate consumption of alcohol without feeling that they have renounced their faith. Boiled down to its simplest expression, being Muslim in the 21st century is an appreciation for one's origins and a reluctance to eat pork.

It is not only non-Muslims who have a partial view of Islam. Muslims, too, have a point of view limited by their own experience. This tunnel vision is often blamed for the radicalization that takes place at the margins of Islam. It is because they do not fully apprehend the diversity and complexity of their faith that some follow the extremist views of preachers of doom and violence. Among those, many are converts, or secularized Muslims who knew and cared little about religion until they embraced radicalism. Conversely, the foundation of deradicalization programs is education: teaching former militants about the complexity of the Islamic tradition, in particular the respect for the law and tolerance of diversity that Prophet Muhammad showed when he was the ruler of Medinah.

Islam in the 21st century is a political religion. There are four Islamic republics, and other states that have made Islam their official religion, bringing Islamic law (Shari'a) in varying degrees into their legal systems. Wherever multiparty elections are held, from Morocco to Indonesia, there are parties representing political Islam. Some blame Islam's political claims for the relative decline of the Muslim world. Once a center of wealth and power and knowledge, it now lags behind its European and East Asian neighbors, still struggling to transition from a rural, agrarian way of life to the urban, now post-industrial age. But for others, only Islam will deliver a successful and indigenous modernization.

Islam is also an economic actor. Shari'a instructs the practices of what is known as Islamic finance, a sector of the international financial system that oversees two trillion dollars worth of assets. For decades now, Islamist organizations have palliated the deficiencies of regional states in the provision of social services, from education to healthcare, counseling, emergency relief, and assistance to find employment. It is the reach of Islamist grassroots networks that has insured the recent electoral success of Islamic parties. Where the Arab Spring brought liberalization and democratization, Islam was given more space in society, not less.

It should be clear to all by now that modernity, and postmodernity, is not absolute convergence toward a single model—call it the Western, secular, democratic model. Islam is not a legacy from a backward past that refuses to die, it is also a claim to shape the future in a new way. Post-communist China is making a similar claim, and there may be others to come, although today none is as forcefully and sometimes as brutally articulated as Islam's. That only would justify the urgency to learn about Islam, deconstruct simplistic stereotypes and educate oneself to the diversity of the world.

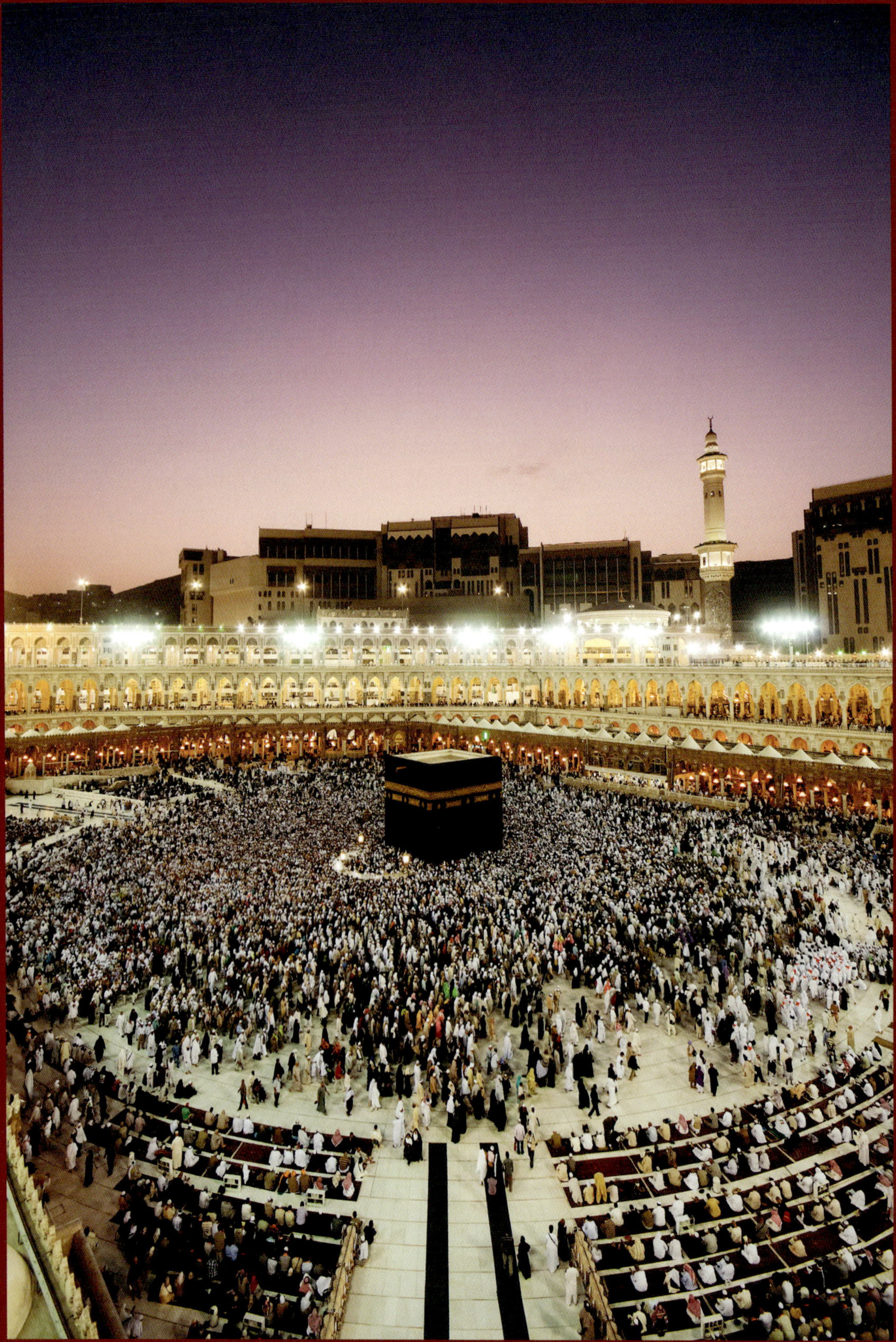

1

Polling the Islamic World

More than 1.6 billion people throughout the world follow the religion called *Islam*, and are therefore known as *Muslims*. Muslims make up about one-fifth of the world's population and live in practically every country in the world. However, most of the world's Muslim population is concentrated in an area that stretches across thousands of miles, from western Africa to the Philippines and China. This region, which includes more than fifty countries, is often referred to as the Islamic world or the Muslim world.

At the center of the Islamic world is the Middle East, which includes the Arabian Peninsula (once called Arabia) where Islam was born about 1,400 years ago. Most Muslims are not Arabs—it is estimated that only about 18 percent of Muslims in the world are Arabs. The majority of Muslims come from non-Arab Asian and African countries. The country with the largest Muslim population is Indonesia, which is thousands of miles to the east of the Arabian Peninsula.

Opposite: Muslims from all over the world circumambulate an ancient shrine, the Kaaba, after completing their dawn prayer in Mecca, Saudi Arabia.

Because Muslims can be found all over the world, there are wide disparities in the ways that Muslims live. Some Muslims are quite wealthy, but many have barely enough to survive. Lifestyle and devotion to religion also varies broadly across the Islamic world. In places like Saudi Arabia and Iran, the people live according to strict religious codes. In Turkey, the lifestyles of many people are similar to that of a typical town in eastern Europe. Muslims speak hundreds of different languages, follow many different customs, wear different styles of clothes, belong to various ethnic groups, and lead many different kinds of lives.

As with most religions and cultures in the world, there are Muslims who see the rules of Islam as strict and others who see them as flexible and accommodating. There are Muslims who follow religious rules carefully, as part of their daily lives, and others who do not closely observe the rules. And there are a few Muslims who believe extreme behavior, including violence, is acceptable, although most others agree it is forbidden.

There is much for westerners to learn about the way Muslims live and the attitudes and opinions of people living in Islamic countries. Since the September 11, 2001, terrorist attacks in which terrorists flew hijacked airliners into the World Trade Center in New York City and the Pentagon near Washington, D.C., there has been a huge interest in learning more about the Muslim world. American public opinion research companies have conducted numerous polls of Muslims in other countries to learn more about what they believe and how they feel about various contemporary issues. The first of these was a landmark study conducted during

Words to Understand in This Chapter

Islam—from an Arabic word meaning "submitted" to God, this is the religion founded by Muhammad in the 7th century CE.

Muslim—a person whose religion is Islam.

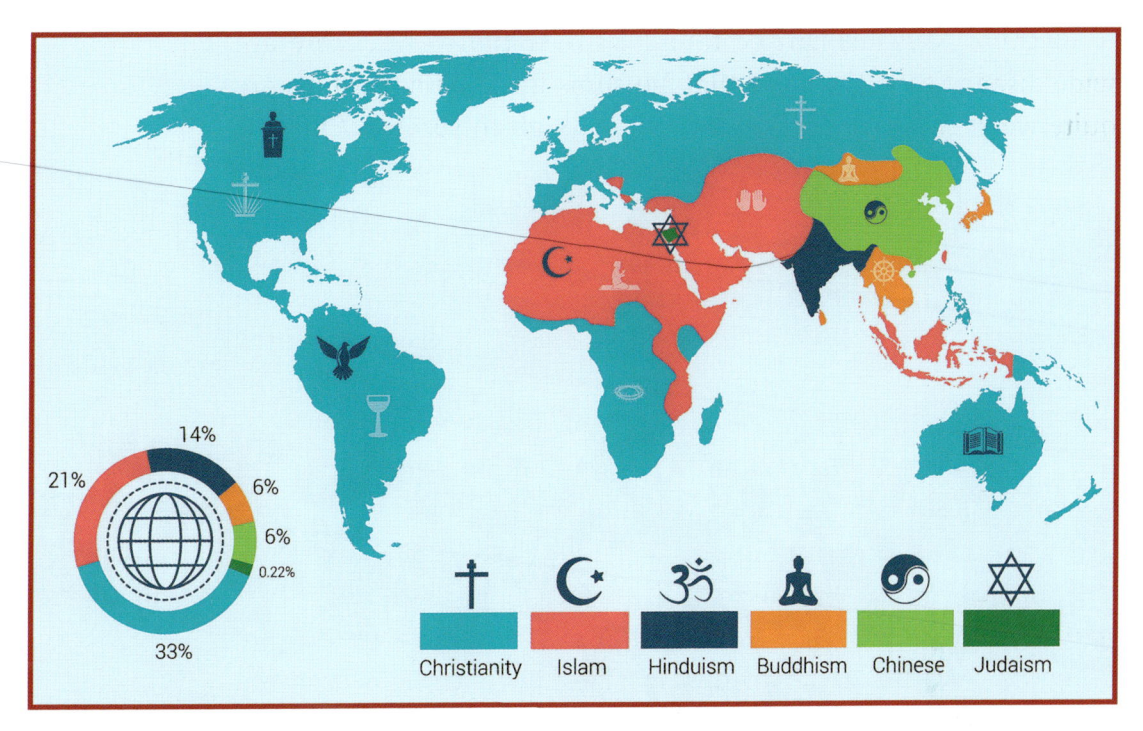

As this map of the world's major religions shows, the largest concentrations of Muslims can be found in the Middle East, North and East Africa, and Central Asia. However, Muslims can be found in every country in the world today.

2001 and 2002 by the Gallup Organization, which interviewed more than 10,000 people in nine predominantly Islamic countries—Indonesia, Iran, Jordan, Kuwait, Lebanon, Morocco, Pakistan, Saudi Arabia, and Turkey. Gallup interviewers asked each person approximately 120 questions about their views on things like politics, culture, and family life. In Iran and Saudi Arabia, both very important Islamic religious centers, this may have been the first time a public-opinion poll was ever taken on these sensitive questions. Gallup's unprecedented study provided interesting insights into the attitudes and beliefs of people throughout the Islamic world.

Over the next six years, Gallup continued to poll the Muslim world, eventually interviewing over 50,000 people. The result was analyzed by scholars that included John L. Esposito, a prominent American expert on Islam, and published in a 2008 book, *Who*

Turks celebrate a festival on the waterfront in Istanbul.

Speaks for Islam: What a Billion Muslims Really Think.

Since then, other public opinion firms have continued to survey the Muslim world. By 2016, the Pew Research Center was regularly surveying the attitudes and opinions of Muslims in thirty-nine different countries and publishing regular reports. The Pew Research Center is a nonpartisan American organization that informs the public about issues, attitudes and trends shaping the world.

Although the number of people interviewed in public opinion surveys is generally only a small fraction of the total global Muslim population of more than 1.6 billion, the people polled in each country were scientifically selected so that the group is representative of the total adult population of that country or region. Therefore, their answers and opinions can be interpreted to help understand the perceptions, hopes, and values of adults across the Islamic world.

Text-Dependent Questions

1. What percentage of Muslims are Arabs.
2. What 2001 event made Americans want to learn more about the Islamic world?

Research Project

Using your school library or the Internet, find out more about the Hashemites, as the descendants of the Prophet Muhammad are known. What is the origin of this clan, and how have they held political and economic power in the Arab world both in ancient times and in the present day?

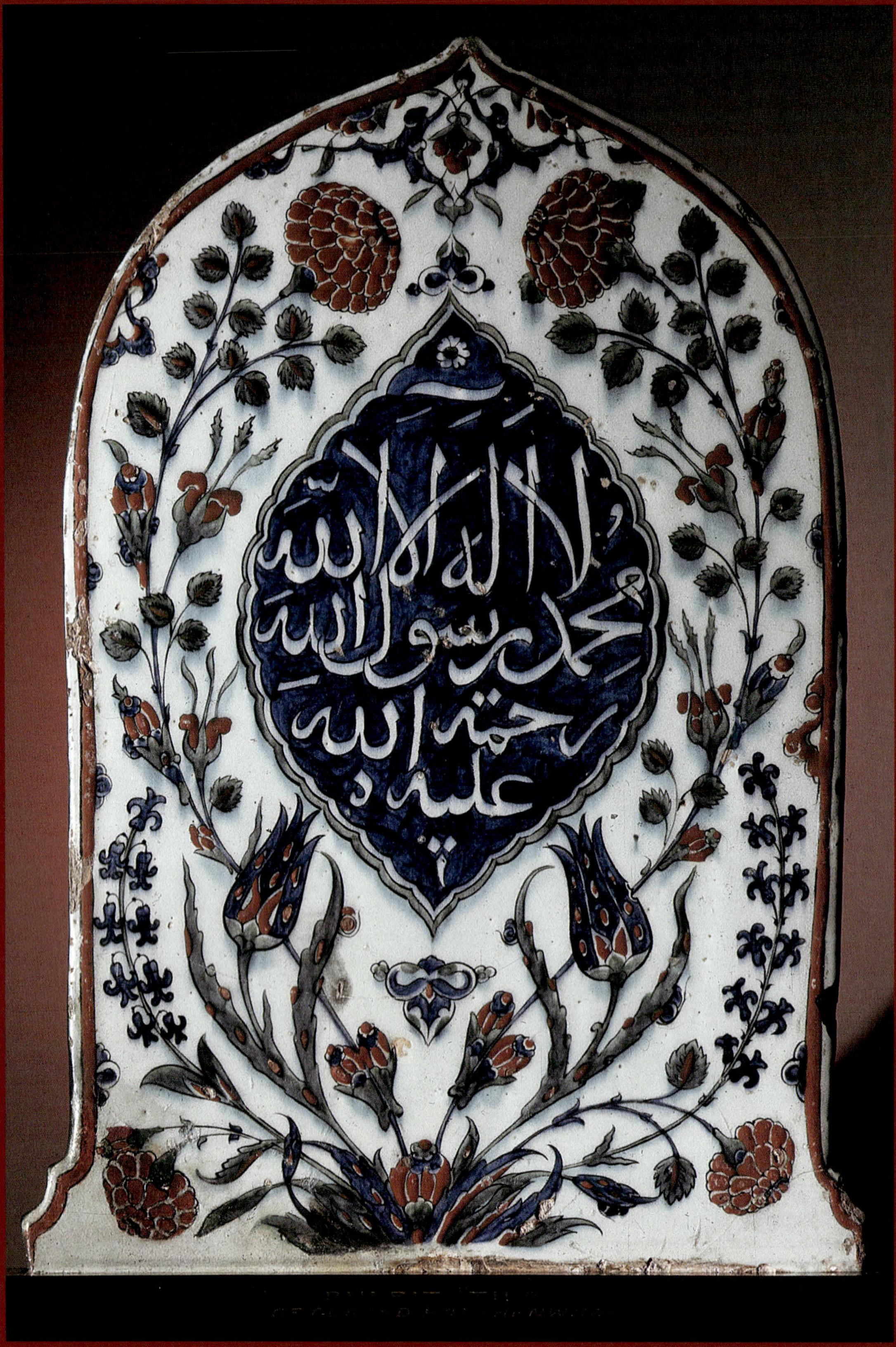
لا اله الا الله
محمد رسول الله
رحمة الله عليه

2

The Roots of the Modern Islamic World

Islam was born early in the seventh century, when a man named Muhammad began to receive messages from *Allah*, or God, through an angel. The word Islam is derived from the Arabic verb aslama, which means "submitted" or "surrendered." Muslims are expected to surrender to the will of Allah.

Muslims believe Allah is the same God worshiped by Jews and Christians. The Arabs trace their lineage from Abraham, an ancient figure also revered by Jews and Christians, and their heritage includes many stories from the Torah and the Old Testament of the Christian Bible. These holy scriptures are also respected by Muslims, although the Islamic holy book, the Qur'an, is revered above them. Muslims consider Muhammad the last in a long line of Abrahamic prophets that includes Isaac, Ishmael, Moses, and Jesus. The messages brought by these prophets were, according to Muslims, misunderstood or distorted by humans, so Allah sent His final, complete message through Muhammad to all humankind.

Opposite: This 17th century Turkish ceramic tile is inscribed with the Muslim creed: "There is no God but Allah and Muhammad is his Prophet."

The Life of Muhammad

Muhammad was an Arab who lived in the city of Mecca (Makka), which is located in modern-day Saudi Arabia. As a child, Muhammad had been orphaned and had grown up tending sheep and goats. He later became a successful trader, although he never learned how to read or write.

In Muhammad's time, the majority of Arabs worshiped many gods. When he was about 40 years old, around 610 CE, Muhammad was meditating in a cave when he was visited by the angel Gabriel. The angel told Muhammad that there is only one god, Allah. Muhammad was ordered to proclaim this message to the people of the Arabian Peninsula.

Muhammad soon began to speak to others as Allah directed. He was very critical of the widespread injustice and oppression that prevailed in Mecca, and the message Muhammad preached from Allah was one of equality, justice, compassion, and mercy.

Words to Understand in This Chapter

Allah—the Arabic word for "God."

caliph—Arabic for "successor." A title held by the spiritual and political leader of all Muslims. This office was said to have expired with the collapse of the Ottoman Empire after the First World War. In 2014 the leader of the Islamic State of Iraq and the Levant (ISIL), Abu Bakr al-Baghdadi, declared himself to be the caliph.

Crusades—a series of invasions of the Middle East by Europeans beginning in the 11th century to seize areas holy to Christians from the hands of Muslims.

mosque—a Muslim house of worship, also known in Arabic as a masjid.

Shiite—one of the 14 percent of Muslims who follows the Shi'a branch of Islam, which began when some early Muslims followed Muhammad's son-in-law Ali as his successor instead of the leader chosen by the rest.

Sunni—a Muslim who belongs to the largest branch of Islam, which holds that Muslims should follow the Sunna, or way, of Muhammad, a tradition that began when the earliest Muslims chose Muhammad's successor.

The Prophet soon attracted a group of committed followers. Most of Muhammad's early followers were poor people and women. Muhammad's message appealed to them because he wanted to establish a community that would treat all of its members fairly and respectfully.

The wealthy and powerful leaders of Mecca opposed Muhammad's message, fearing that it threatened their livelihoods. They persecuted Muhammad and his followers, passing laws that prohibited all business and social relations between Muslims and non-Muslims. The Meccans took away Muslim homes and properties. As a result, Muslims living in Mecca could not earn a living, and some starved to death.

At the same time, the Meccans targeted and tortured Muslims, especially those who were poor and powerless. Some Muslims were attacked and murdered during this time of unrest. Meccan leaders also plotted to kill Muhammad and his prominent followers, but these plots failed. Ultimately, this oppression forced the Muslims to begin looking for a new home outside of Mecca.

In 620 representatives from Yathrib, an oasis community in Arabia approximately 250 miles north of Mecca, asked Muhammad to come to their city and settle their disputes. Two tribes of the region, Aws and Khazraj, had been engaged in violent warfare for many years, and wanted Muhammad to help them resolve their differences. In 622, after the plot to assassinate Muhammad was uncovered, Muhammad and the Muslims left Mecca and moved to Yathrib. This important event is known as the *hijra*, from an Arabic word meaning to migrate or to leave one's tribe.

In the Arab world of the seventh century, this was a major decision. The tribe was the basis of Arab society. Members of a tribe considered themselves bound by moral and social obligations in addition to family ties. When Muhammad and his followers left Mecca, they abandoned their responsibilities to other members of their tribe. The relatives they left behind in Mecca vowed to destroy the Muslims who had rejected their families and traditions.

When Muhammad arrived in Yathrib, he helped the feuding tribal leaders settle their differences. Then the Prophet and his companions established the first Muslim community (*umma*). The first **mosque** was built next to Muhammad's house, and it became

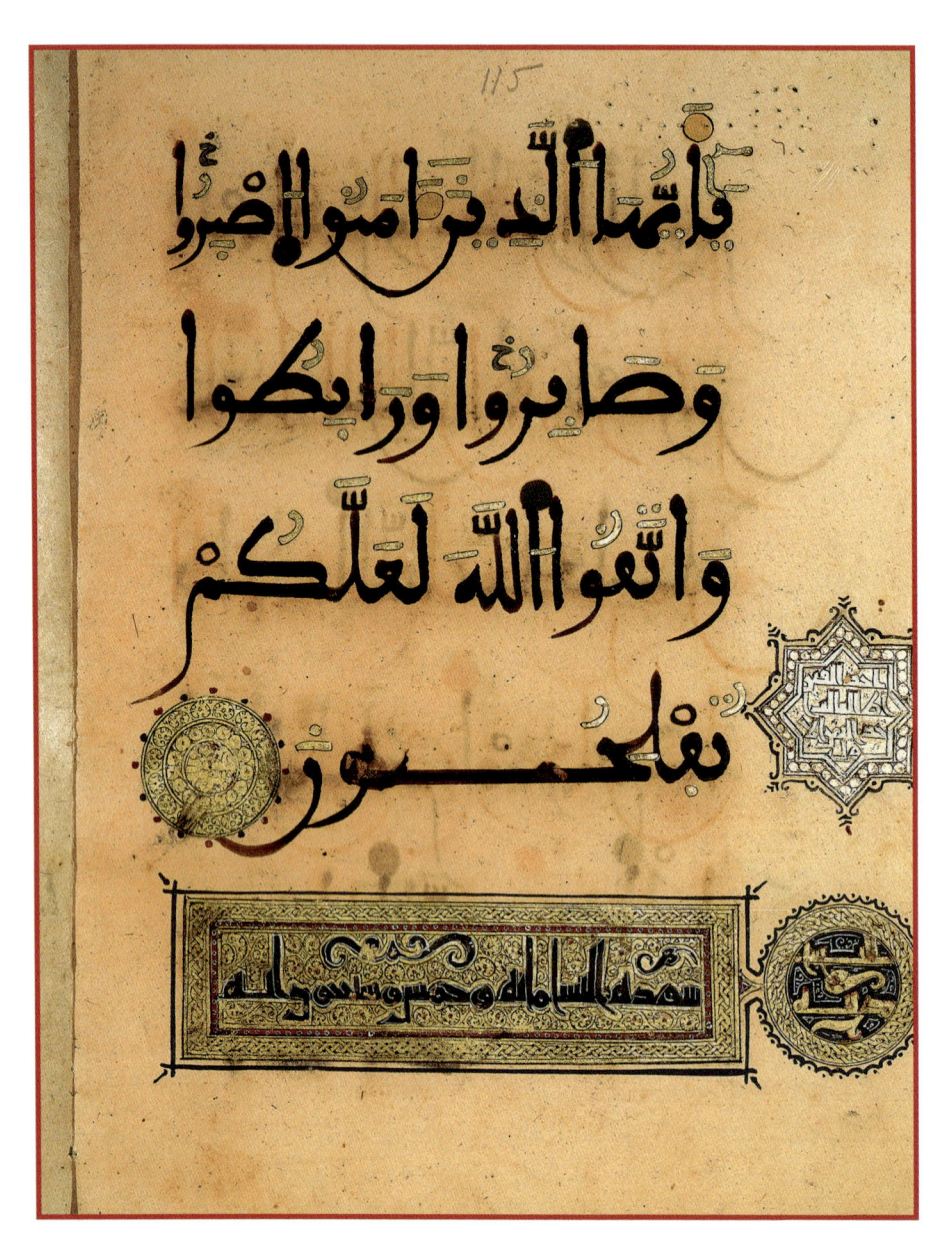

An ornate page from a copy of the Qur'an that dates back to the 13th century. The verse shown in Arabic here reads, "O ye who believe, persevere in patience and constancy."

the center of religious and social activity for the Muslims. Even though Muhammad did not force any of the city's inhabitants to convert to Islam, many people chose to become Muslims. Islamic ideas soon became the basis of the city's judicial and social systems. The name of the city was eventually changed to Medina (which means "city," but has been interpreted to mean "city of the Prophet").

In Islamic thought the *umma* is the basis of all social relations. Membership in the *umma* is more binding than membership in a family or tribe. Members of the *umma* must protect and defend each other regardless of their previous tribal relations. This pact of mutual defense applied to the entire community—Muslim and non-Muslim. If any group within the *umma* was threatened, the rest of the *umma* was obligated to defend them. The concept of *umma* supplanted the traditional Arab notion of obligations based on blood relationships. Acceptance of this new social ideal was an important act of faith for the Muslims and for the non-Muslims who lived among them in Medina.

The Muslims at Medina and their allies were at war with the Meccans from 624 to 628, when a peace treaty was negotiated. In 629 the Meccans broke the treaty and the war resumed. The fighting ended in 630 when Muhammad led an army of 10,000 Muslims and their allies to Mecca. Disheartened, outnumbered, and surrounded, the Meccans surrendered without a fight. After the conquest of Mecca, many people living in the city decided to become Muslims. Muhammad continued to teach the messages revealed from Allah until he died peacefully two years later.

On the Arabian Peninsula at the time of the Prophet, information was preserved primarily through memorization, rather than writing. During Muhammad's lifetime, many of his companions memorized his teachings verbatim. In the years after Muhammad's death, these teachings were written down and organized as the Qur'an—the holy book of Islam. The early Muslims went to great lengths to preserve the exact wording and organization of Allah's teachings, and Muslims believe the text of the Qur'an is the literal, unchanged word of Allah, given through Muhammad, his prophet and messenger. The Qur'an explains what is required to be a Muslim and to live a good life. Although the holy book has been translated into English and other languages, Muslims maintain that the Qur'an can only be truly understood when read in Arabic. Even today, many Muslims memorize the entire Qur'an.

The Rapid Spread of a New Religion

After Muhammad's death, his followers gathered huge armies, first conquering all the Arabs and then defeating many surrounding nations. The Muslims won nearly every battle, and in a remarkably short period they established a vast empire that stretched from Spain in the west to China in the east. The Muslims felt that Allah blessed and supported their efforts. This sentiment is supported by the Qur'an, which consistently told Muslims not to fear or worry because Allah was with them and would give them victory if they were true believers.

The Muslims wanted to spread their religion throughout the world, as Allah commanded. As the Arab armies won victories, they offered the vanquished peoples an opportunity to convert to Islam. This conversion was supposed to be a free decision. The Qur'an says that non-Muslims cannot be forcibly converted, and gives Jews and Christians, known as *ahl al-kitab* ("the people of the book") or *ahl al-dhimma* ("the protected people"), more respect than followers of other religions, because these two groups worship the same God that Muslims worship. The people of the book who wanted to continue following their faiths were given certain rights in the Islamic state, and were required to pay a tax in return. However, many people living under Muslim rule eventually adopted Islam.

It is worth noting that the spread of Islam was driven by more than just military conquest. The enlightened Islamic culture was attractive to many people, particularly when compared to the repressive and at times barbaric systems of thought that had pre-

A Shiite bows his head in prayer. A schism in the Muslim community occurred after the death of Ali, the fourth caliph, in 661 and the massacre of his son Hussein at the Battle of Karbala in 680.

vailed in other parts of the region at the time. In some areas, trade and the exchange of goods and ideas played a more central role in the spread of the religion than did warfare, particularly as Islam spread into Asia.

The Islamic empire contained many great cities, some with impressive libraries, universities, monuments, and public buildings, and harbored people of many different cultures, including Roman, Greek, Persian, Jewish, and Hindu. The Muslims absorbed the knowledge and culture of many of these peoples and combined them with their own traditions to form new civilizations. They made many new advances in architecture, science, medicine, and mathematics. Europeans learned a great deal from Muslim societies. For instance, the symbols we use to represent numbers today (1, 2, 3, etc.) were borrowed from the Arabic mathematical system. Muslim intellectuals also preserved many ancient books about philosophy and science by translating them into Arabic. The most important of these books are those of Plato, Aristotle, and Plotinus.

Division of Muslims into Sects

An important event in Islamic history is the division of Muslims into two major groups. This schism became a source of conflict that pitted Muslim against Muslim, and differences between the two groups persist today.

After Muhammad's death, his followers disagreed about who would lead the Muslims. One group believed that the succession of leadership should be hereditary, and wanted to choose a leader from Muhammad's family. They supported Muhammad's son-in-law, Ali, to be the Muslim leader. Most Muslims, however, believed that the leader should be a person of great faith chosen from the Muslim community, and selected a man named Abu Bakr to be the first *khalifa* (**caliph**, or "successor"). This indicated that succession would be based on the piety of the leader, rather than on heredity.

Ali was eventually elected caliph in 656, but he was assassinated in 661. Ali's supporters claimed that his son Hussein should become caliph. However, Hussein and a group of his followers were massacred at the Battle of Karbala in 680. This smaller group of Muslims who followed Ali and his family became known as **Shiites**. The name *Shiite* comes from the Arabic word *shia*, meaning party. In time, the word came to be used primarily in connection with Ali. Thus, Shiites came to mean the party or followers of Ali. The larger group of Muslims are known as **Sunni**, from an Arabic word meaning "the path," because they follow the path they believe Muhammad set for them.

Today, about 85 percent of Muslims are Sunnis, while about 14 percent are Shiites. Many Shiites live in Iran, Iraq, Lebanon, and Bahrain; there are smaller populations in Syria, Pakistan, India, and Azerbaijan. Although Sunnis and Shiites disagree about the leadership of the Muslim nation, the members of both groups obey the Qur'an and follow the principles of Islam.

Crusades and Colonialism

In the eighth century Muslim armies had moved from Africa across the Mediterranean Sea into Spain, and by the eleventh century they had created an enlightened civilization there. At the same time, Muslim forces were expanding their territories into Eastern Europe as well. In 1095 the leader of the Roman Catholic Church, Pope Urban II, called on European rulers to send armies east to

A Medieval manuscript illustration shows a ship crossing the Mediterranean Sea carrying European knights to fight in the Middle East. The Crusades were a series of wars between Muslims and Christians that occured from 1095 to 1291.

protect Constantinople, a city in modern-day Turkey that was the center of the Christian Byzantine Empire. Another goal was the capture of Jerusalem from the Muslims, because of the city's religious significance to Christians. The pope's call marked the start of the **Crusades**, a series of invasions by Europeans into territory controlled by Muslims. The invasions continued until the thirteenth century.

Thousands of European knights responded to the call, marching east to Constantinople. Some of them joined the First Crusade for religious reasons, but many participated because they saw an opportunity to seize new lands and increase their personal wealth. By 1099 the Crusaders had fought their way to Jerusalem, capturing it and other cities from the Muslims.

The European knights established small Crusader kingdoms from which they ruled the conquered territory, but Muslims based in Egypt later counterattacked and took back Jerusalem. Over the next two centuries a series of wars in the region pitted Christians against Muslims (and sometimes European Christians against Orthodox Christians living in the Byzantine empire). The Muslims eventually regained control of their Arab territories, but the power of the Arab caliphs was severely weakened.

In the West, the Crusades are often viewed in a positive light, as a glorious struggle to take control over the Holy Land. Muslims view the Crusades in a much different way—as an offensive, unprovoked invasion motivated by a religious fanaticism bent on destroying the Islamic faith. Muslims vividly recall atrocities committed by European knights, such as the massacre of Muslim and Jewish civilians after Jerusalem was captured in 1099, and the murder of 2,700 prisoners by the army of the English king Richard the Lionhearted in 1191.

Even today the Crusades remind Muslims of the danger posed by the West. Although the word "crusade" is often used to refer to a struggle, to Muslim ears the word connotes a religious war against Islam. For example, when President George W. Bush described his government's renewed effort to combat terrorism as a "crusade" shortly after the September 11, 2001, terrorist attacks on the United States, many Muslims were offended. They believed the president was calling for a crusade against their religion, rather than against extremists willing to use terrorism as a political tool.

The spread of European influence after the fifteenth century had an even greater effect on the Islamic world. By the eighteenth and nineteenth centuries, countries like Great Britain, France, Italy, the Netherlands, and Germany had established colonies throughout Africa, Asia, and the Middle East. The Muslims living in the colonies were often discriminated against by their European rulers. The resources of Muslim lands contributed to the growth of the empire, but the European powers did little to help the lives of ordinary people living in their colonies.

When the Ottoman Empire, a large Muslim empire based in Turkey, collapsed at the end of World War I, Britain and France took control of the former Ottoman territories. During the war these two countries had made the secret Sykes-Picot agreement, which divided the Middle East into British and French spheres of influence. The European powers controlled the territories by supporting leaders who followed the policies the French or British imposed. People living in these countries had little input into their government.

During the 1920s and 1930s, independence movements emerged in many of these colonies. The oppressed residents of the colonies protested against their colonial rulers, and these protests at times became violent. Some of these territories became independent in the 1930s; others won their freedom during or after World War II, when the European powers had been weakened by the global struggle. However, the western colonial powers had created their states in Africa and the Middle East by imposing arbitrary borders, which often separated people of similar ethnic backgrounds or religious beliefs. In some places, old enemies were joined together or the colonial rulers had favored one group over another. Once the states gained independence, disputes erupted.

Western involvement in the Islamic world continued even after

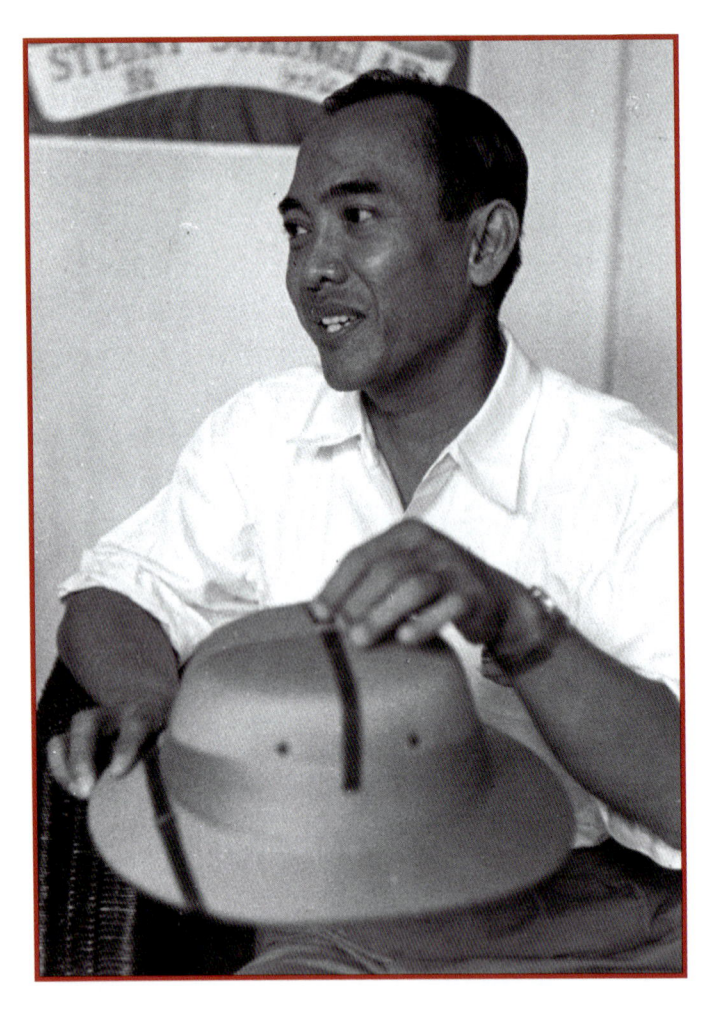

Achmad Sukarno (1902–1970) was the first president of Indonesia after the country became independent in August 1945. During his rule the communist party gradually gained greater power in Indonesia. In the mid-1960s, the US Central Intelligence Agency (CIA) orchestrated a coup that allowed General Suharto, who held pro-American views, to seize power.

countries like Indonesia, Algeria, India, Lebanon, and Jordan gained their independence. The United States and European countries sent money, weapons, technology, and occasionally military forces to these countries. Western goals included protecting their access to the Middle East's vast reserves of petroleum and preventing the Soviet Union from gaining influence in the Islamic world. Although the US and some other Western governments claimed that they wanted to promote freedom and democracy in these countries, in reality they often supported oppressive dictators who favored the West. In some cases, the US was secretly involved in removing leaders with popular support, such as Iranian Prime Minister Mohammed Mossadegh, who was overthrown in a CIA-supported coup in 1953, and Indonesian President Achmad Sukarno, who was removed from power in the mid-1960s.

The involvement of the West created or worsened a number of conflicts in the Islamic world. This history has caused many Muslims to distrust the West and believe that the United States and other western nations want to dominate Islamic countries.

Since gaining their independence, the people of a few Muslim countries have enjoyed more freedom and a better life. However, many Muslims have suffered as dictators used military power or the threat of harsh punishments to take control. Other governments have been unable or unwilling to stop fighting between groups inside their countries, or to protect one group from hurting another, or to help their people get better education, jobs, or living conditions. Many problems and conflicts remain for Muslims to solve.

Text-Dependent Questions

1. What are some things that Europeans learned from Muslim societies?
2. What are the two major sects within Islam?
3. How do Europeans feel about the Crusades, a series of wars fought between 1095 and 1291? How does this opinion differ from the Muslim view of the Crusades?

Research Project

The division of Islam into Sunni and Shia branches dates back to the seventh century. Using your school library or the Internet, find out more about Ali, Muhammad's son-in-law and companion who became the fourth caliph in 656 ce. Write a two-page report about Ali, and how his assassination in 661 led to the Sunni-Shia split. Include some examples of how these two Muslim sects have clashed throughout history, to the present day.

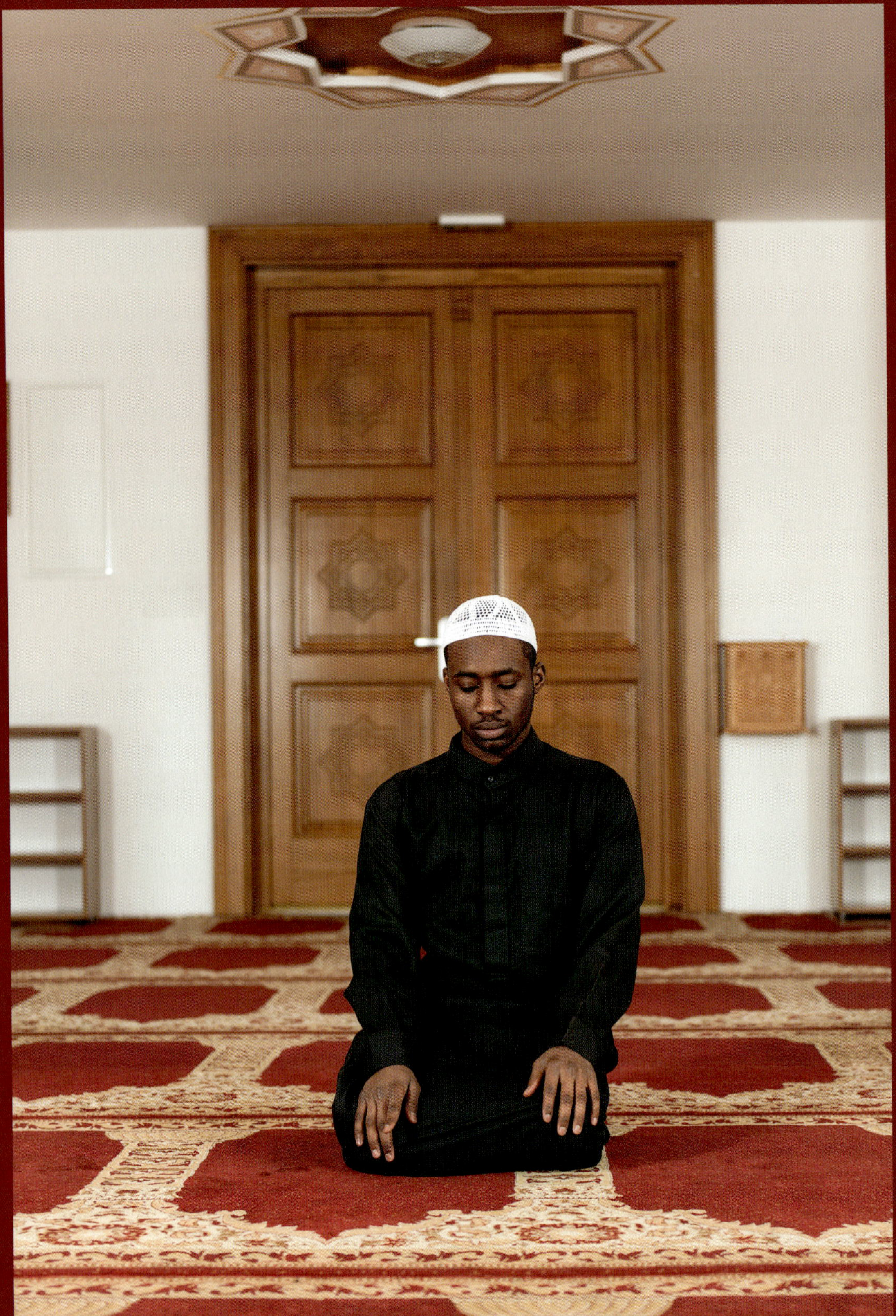

3

What it Means to be a Muslim Today

The followers of Islam are expected to live every day according to their faith. The Qur'an and other texts based on the sayings and deeds of Muhammad tell Muslims to be honest, respectful, faithful to their spouses, and helpful to the poor or weak.

With a few exceptions, there are no priests or ministers in Islam to instruct the faithful or speak on behalf of Allah. To become a Muslim and fulfill the faith, one simply obeys the commandments of the Qur'an. Throughout the Islamic world, these requirements guide the rhythm of life for millions of people every day.

The Five Pillars of Islam

The most important requirement in Islam is a belief in one God. There are five important precepts that are observed by all Muslims, known as the five pillars of Islam. The first of these is the simplest: A Muslim announces in Arabic Allah's uniqueness and Muhammad's

Opposite: An African Muslim performs one of his daily prayers. The Qur'an and the example of Muhammad's life guide Muslims in proper behavior, including the requirement to pray five times a day.

29

being a messenger before witnesses who are also Muslims. The announcement is the basic message of Islam, one that every Muslim learns from a very early age: *La ilah illa Allah Muhammad rasul Allah*. This means, "There is no god but Allah, and Muhammad is His messenger."

The second pillar unites Muslims across the world in a ritual that Muslims have had to practice every day since Muhammad's time. At different times during the day—usually at dawn, midday, afternoon, evening, and before bedtime—Muslims are supposed to stop whatever they are doing and pray.

Muslims may pray with others in a mosque (a place of worship) or in their home or office, or even on the sidewalk. The only time Muslim men (and according to some interpretations, Muslim women) are required to pray in a mosque is at mid-day prayers every Friday. Males and females usually pray in separate areas of a mosque.

Cleanliness during prayer is important, and Muslims perform a ritual wash (or ablution) before reciting each of the five required prayers. If the Muslim is not at home or in a mosque, he or she may place a rug on the ground wherever they are and pray on it. Worshippers remove their shoes before prayer, and on Fridays a large collection of shoes can pile up at the entrance to the prayer area.

To pray, Muslims kneel and then bow their heads to touch the floor several times, always in the direction of Mecca. The prayers

Words to Understand in This Chapter

Eid al-Fitr—a holiday feast that marks the end of Ramadan.
Islamist—a Muslim activist who wants to make Islam the center of social and political life in Islamic countries.
Ramadan—the ninth month in the Islamic calendar when Muslims refrain from eating or drinking during daylight hours.

and the movements are the same for every Muslim, and when they are praying in a group, Muslims kneel and bow as a group, following the *imam* (prayer leader) who signals each movement by saying *Allahu Akhbar* ("God is greatest").

By tradition, Muslims never make paintings or statues that depict Allah or figures like Muhammad, so that Muslims will not forget that they worship only Allah. Intricate geometric designs and beautiful calligraphic writings adorn the walls of most large mosques. Smaller mosques, especially in the West, cannot afford such decorations and appear simpler.

In Muslim cities and towns across the world, the voice of the *mu'adhdhin* can be heard chanting a call to prayer from the tower of the local mosque at each prayer time. The five required prayers are an important part of a Muslim's day.

Islamic law does not permit Allah to be depicted in drawings, paintings, sculpture, or other artwork. Representations of Muhammad are generally also forbidden; some Muslims believe the human figure itself should never be depicted. Images or icons of Allah, Muhammad, or the saints could lead some people to worship them as idols, a practice strictly forbidden in Islam. Because of the restrictions, over the centuries Muslim artists focused their creativity in other ways, such as the creation of decorative tile patterns and ornate calligraphy.

The third pillar requires Muslims to give to the poor, orphans, widows, or others less fortunate than themselves. Some Islamic countries, such as Pakistan, collect a tax to fulfill this requirement. In other countries, this religious tax is left to the individual Muslims to pay according to their consciences.

The fourth pillar is perhaps the most difficult. For the entire month of **Ramadan**, the ninth month of the Islamic lunar calendar, all Muslims except young children, nursing mothers, travelers, or the sick must abstain from eating, drinking, and other earthly pleasures from sunrise to sunset. The fast during Ramadan honors the month when Muhammad received his first messages from Allah. Ramadan is a time for Muslims to be thankful for what they have, renew their spirit, and make peace with others.

The final pillar is the *hajj*, or pilgrimage to Mecca. Every Muslim is expected to visit the holy city at least once during his or her lifetime, if they are able to make the trip physically and financially. Before air travel made the journey to Mecca easier, Muslims might spend years traveling thousands of miles to reach Mecca.

Muslim pilgrims perform a ritual on Mount Arafat during the annual *hajj* pilgrimage.

Now more than a million people visit each year. Non-Muslims, however, are forbidden from entering most of Mecca.

Muslims making the pilgrimage wear plain white garments. Everyone is considered to be equal regardless of their wealth or background—even kings and queens wear the same simple clothes as the other pilgrims and live alongside them. While in Mecca, pilgrims do not shave, comb their hair, cut their nails, or wear perfume. By following the same simple lifestyle, the pilgrims stress their unity as Muslims and are reminded that earthly things like wealth and appearance are not very important. They express unity by the sameness of life that they lead in those few days. The simplicity of that life indicates their view of earthly things.

The rituals of the *hajj* last for several days. They include walking seven times around a small building called the Kaaba. The Kaaba is shaped like a cube (the word *kaaba* means "cube" in Arabic) and covered with a black cloth. It has no windows and nothing inside. The Kaaba is located in the center of an outdoor courtyard the size of a football field in the Great Mosque of Mecca. Muslims believe Adam, the first man, built the Kaaba as a place of worship, and that the building was later repaired by Abraham and his son Ishmael. An ancient black stone, called al-Hajar al-Aswad, is located in the eastern wall of the Kaaba. According to one legend, the stone was originally white when it was given to Adam after his fall from Paradise, but it turned black from absorbing the sins of the millions of pilgrims who have touched it over the centuries. Another legend is that the stone was sent from heaven to Abraham—possibly it was a meteorite—and placed in the wall as a marker for pilgrims to determine how many times they had walked around the Kaaba. After the pilgrims have circled the Kaaba seven times, some kiss the stone.

The rituals of the *hajj* are intended to emphasize the unity of Muslims, and to confirm and strengthen the unity of the Abrahamic faiths. This is an important part of the Muslim creed. Muhammad is considered the last in a long line of Abrahamic prophets. The rituals of pilgrimage repeatedly underscore the

Muslim belief in the divinity of the messages of all the Abrahamic prophets and the basic unity of those who follow the creed of Abraham.

For nearly every Muslim who makes the trip, the *hajj* is a life-changing event. People from all nations and races, rich and poor, become equals when they travel to Mecca. Making the journey reminds them of the importance of faith in their lives and the need to respect their fellow Muslims. "Elsewhere, except at the best of times, every person looked out for himself," writes Michael Wolfe, an American Muslim who went on a *hajj* in 1990. "During the *Hajj*, people looked out for each other."

The government of Saudi Arabia, where Mecca is located, provides transportation, shelter, food, and guides to help the pilgrims through the rituals. This is an enormous task during the special *hajj* season that occurs for one week each year, when hundreds of thousands of visitors flood the city. Some visitors have died in the crush of the crowds at holy places, from the heat, or owing to other disasters.

Other Requirements of Islam

A Muslim's duties extend beyond the five pillars. Islam requires believers to show their obedience to Allah in every aspect of life. Some of these social and moral requirements come from the Qur'an. Others are derived from things Muhammad said, actions he took, and even things he did not do. These are known as the Sunna ("custom" or "way") of the Prophet, and include collections of Muhammad's statements, which are called the *Hadith*. Using the Sunna, Muslims can follow Muhammad's example of a near-perfect life and understand the Qur'an better. The Hadith reports were compiled from the memories of Muhammad's followers after he died. (The word *Hadith* can refer to one or more of the reports about Muhammad's Sunna.)

Muslims disagree about the accuracy of some of the Hadith. Sunni and Shiite Muslims have different opinions on how

Muslims should behave, and which Hadith are legitimate. Because Sunni Muslims are the largest sect, this section will focus on Sunni beliefs and traditions.

The Qur'an tells believers, "Those who surrender themselves to God and accept the true Faith; who are devout, sincere, patient, humble, charitable, and chaste; who fast and are ever mindful of God—on these, both men and women, God will bestow forgiveness and a rich reward." (33: 35). This and other passages in the Qur'an, along with similar ones in the Sunna, call on Muslims to live morally upstanding lives. Muslims are expected to give to the poor and to orphaned children, to be courteous to others, to be honest and trustworthy, to refrain from gambling or drinking alcohol, and to defend Islam from attackers. Muslims also value hospitality. Guests to a family's home, whether close friends or strangers, receive food, drink, and high respect.

One of the most visible symbols of Muslim life are the veils that many Muslim women wear in public. These sometimes cover their entire bodies, including their faces. The Qur'an calls on Muslim women to dress modestly. Many Muslim women wear a simple head scarf that covers their hair but not their faces. Other women, particularly those living in countries like Saudi Arabia and Yemen, may wear a full-body robe with only slits for the eyes. Others wear various kinds of veils that cover all or part of their faces. Still other women wear nothing on their faces or hair, or cover their hair only during prayers and in a mosque. Men are also supposed to dress modestly and in many Muslim societies men may wear caps or turbans as signs of their religious devotion.

Islam teaches its followers to enjoy life and its pleasures as gifts from Allah, as long as they remember that the true reward for a good life comes after death.

Holidays and Celebrations

Muslims observe certain celebrations every year with holidays and feasts. They track their holidays by the Islamic calendar, which follows the phases of the moon rather than the circuit of the sun around the earth. Like the Gregorian calendar used in the West, a year in the Islamic calendar includes twelve months; however, because the cycles of the moon and the sun do not quite match, the Islamic year is about eleven days shorter than the 365-day Western year.

The Islamic calendar begins in the year Muhammad left Mecca for Medina (622 CE in the Western calendar). Nearly all Muslim countries follow the western calendar for business but use the Islamic calendar to determine the dates of religious holidays.

The most important month of the Islamic calendar is Ramadan. Because the Muslim calendar is based on the movement of the moon instead of the sun, Ramadan occurs in different

Malaysian Muslims weigh and divide the meat of a slaughtered cow as part of the Eid al-Adha celebration. During this festival, Muslim families are required to slaughter a sheep, cow, goat, or other livestock, and share a portion of the meat with the poor members of their community.

seasons in different years. When it falls in summer, the wait for nightfall and the breaking of the fast are more difficult because summer days are longer.

When Ramadan is officially over, Muslims greet the end of the fasting with a joyful feast called **Eid al-Fitr** that may last up to three days. They celebrate the holiday by visiting friends and relatives, as well as the graves of loved ones who have died. They give gifts to their family and to poor people.

Another feast, Eid al-Adha, marks the high point of the month when most Muslims visit Mecca on a pilgrimage. The Muslims visiting Mecca sacrifice an animal on this day as part of their *hajj* ritual. Muslims everywhere else in the world join them by slaughtering a goat, sheep, or other animal to begin the feast. They share the meat with friends, relatives, and the needy.

Muslims in different parts of the world celebrate other annual holidays, such as the birthday of Muhammad and New Year's Day on the Islamic calendar. Shiites mourn the death of Ali's son Hussein, who was murdered in Karbala. They wear mourning clothes, visit the gravesites of important Shiite leaders, and read stories about their fallen ancestors.

The Islamic calendar follows the same seven-day week as the Gregorian calendar. Although Friday is the day of congregational prayer, it is not considered a day of rest to Muslims, like Sunday is to Christians or the Sabbath (Saturday) is to Jews. Still, Muslims in many countries do not work on Fridays, and some countries require businesses and government offices to close on that day of the week.

Islamic Law

In the early centuries following the death of Muhammad, Muslims established religious rules for living, called Sharia. Sharia is a legal system based on the Qur'an and three other sources: written narrations about Muhammad's deeds and sayings, the religious scholars' opinions, and analogical reasoning.

Islamic law gives rights and freedom to Muslims as well as rules to follow, and it can change with the times. *Sharia* does not simply say which acts are right and which are wrong—some are only encouraged, discouraged, or simply allowed. In those cases, an individual must decide how to act based on the circumstances.

When Islamic law was created, religion was the only source of the rules governing society. The concept of separating church and state developed much later. Today, most Islamic countries have adopted civil law or common law systems to regulate their societies, and limit *Sharia* to personal and family laws. Countries like Saudi Arabia and Iran purport to base all of their laws on *Sharia*. Countries like Egypt, Syria, Jordan, Iraq, Algeria, Morocco, Tunisia, and Kuwait have adopted the French civil law system, while Pakistan, Sudan, and Indonesia mix Islamic law with the British common law system.

The level of freedom a Muslim enjoys often depends greatly on the rulers of their country. The United States and many western nation-states are democracies in which people have the power to choose their leaders and speak their minds. Only a few Islamic countries give their people a degree of democracy similar to that enjoyed by people in the West.

A 2012 Pew Research Center survey of six Arab countries, plus Turkey and Pakistan, found that most Muslims in this region believe democracy is the best form of government. A majority of Muslims in Lebanon, Turkey, Egypt, Tunisia, and Jordan, as well as a plurality in Pakistan, do not simply support the general notion of democracy, they also embrace specific features of a democratic system, such as competitive elections and free speech.

However, it's important to note that Muslims in these countries do not view the United States as promoting democracy in the Middle East. This view, of course, is contrary to a view held by most Americans that US policies are helpful in spreading democracy and greater freedom.

The 2012 Pew study also indicated that a substantial number of Muslims would like to see their religion have an important role in

Which Is More Important?

	Strong Economy	Good Democracy
Turkey	37%	58%
Lebanon	46%	53%
Egypt	49%	48%
Tunisia	59%	40%
Pakistan	58%	34%
Jordan	61%	33%

Source: Pew Research Center, July 2012

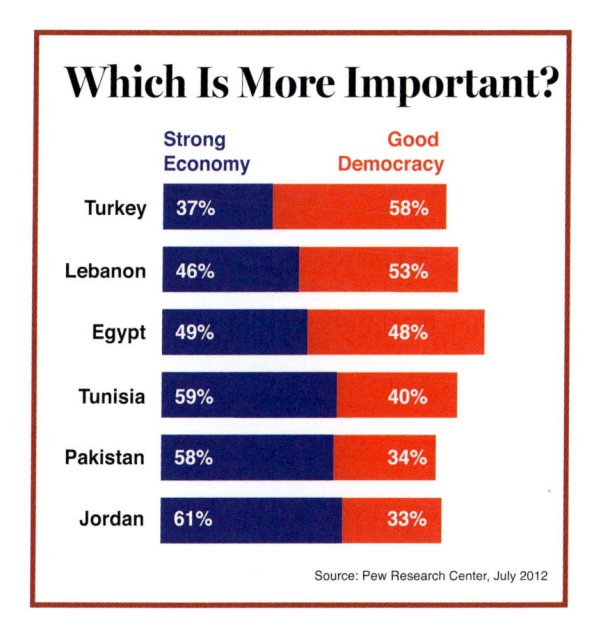

the political affairs of the nation-state in which they live. However, there are significant differences over the degree to which the legal system should be based on Islamic law, or Sharia. A majority of those polled in Pakistan, Jordan, and Egypt said laws should strictly follow the teachings of the Quran. However, a majority of Tunisians and a 44 percent plurality of Turks said they would prefer laws to be influenced by the values and principles of Islam, but not strictly follow the Quran. The finding in Turkey goes along with the historical reality that the modern state was established on secular principles in 1923. However, in recent years the government of Recep Tayyip Erdogan has pursued some policies that can be described as moderately Islamist.

A subsequent Pew Research Center study conducted in 2013 found strong support for making Sharia the official law of their country. In Muslim-majority countries across South Asia, Southeast Asia, sub-Saharan Africa, and the Middle East-North Africa region most people said they wanted Sharia to become their country's official legal code.

In South Asia, the idea of making Sharia the official law received extremely high support among Muslims in Afghanistan (99 percent), Pakistan (84 percent), and Bangladesh (82 percent). The percentage of Muslims who say they favor making Islamic law the official law in their country was nearly as high across the Southeast Asian countries surveyed—86 percent in Malaysia, 77 percent in Thailand, and 72 percent in Indonesia.

In sub-Saharan Africa, at least half of Muslims in most countries surveyed said they favored making Sharia the official law of the land, including Niger (86 percent), Djibouti (82 percent), the Democratic Republic of the Congo (74 percent) and Nigeria (71 percent). In

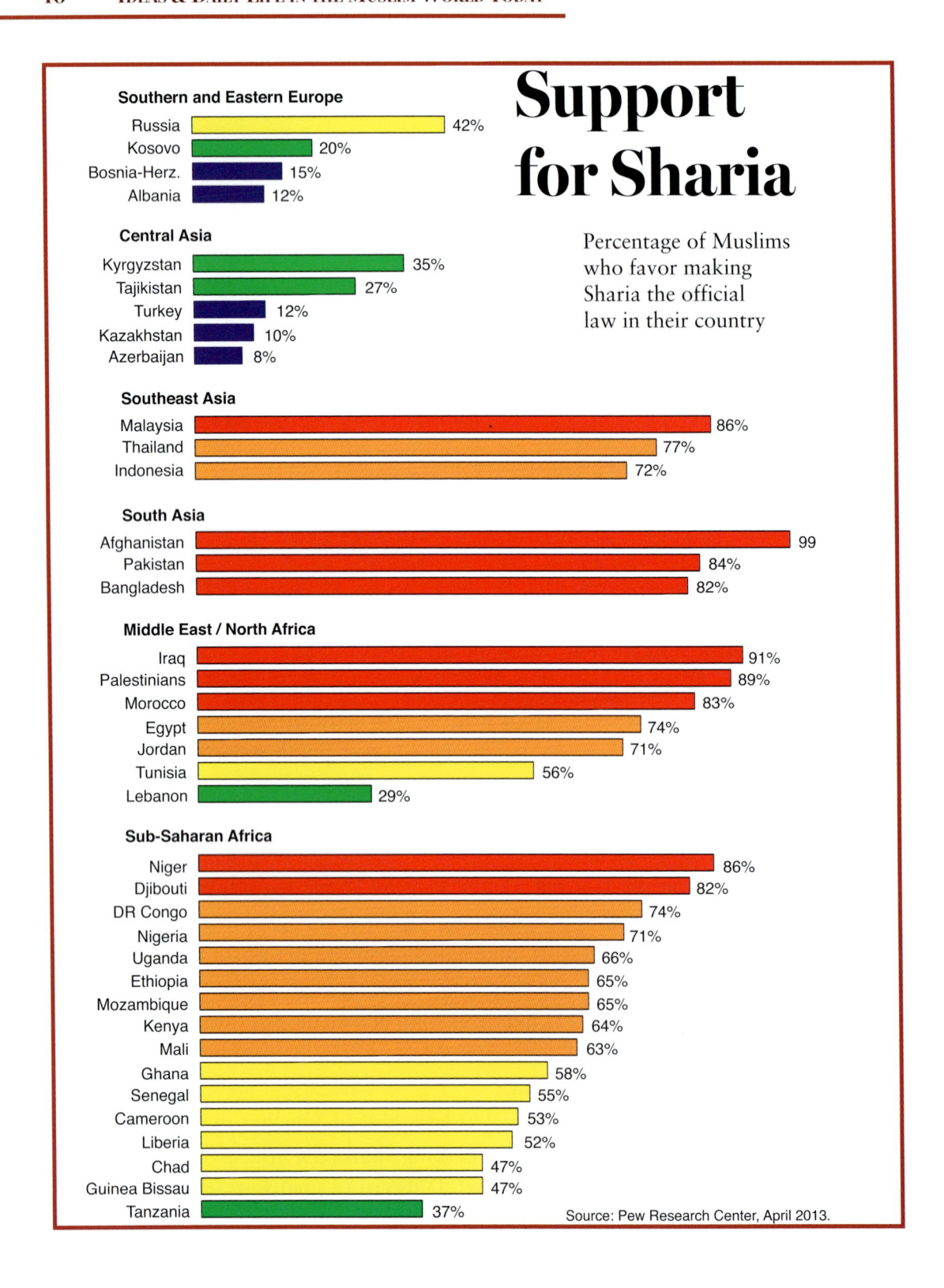

Support for Sharia

Percentage of Muslims who favor making Sharia the official law in their country

Southern and Eastern Europe
- Russia: 42%
- Kosovo: 20%
- Bosnia-Herz.: 15%
- Albania: 12%

Central Asia
- Kyrgyzstan: 35%
- Tajikistan: 27%
- Turkey: 12%
- Kazakhstan: 10%
- Azerbaijan: 8%

Southeast Asia
- Malaysia: 86%
- Thailand: 77%
- Indonesia: 72%

South Asia
- Afghanistan: 99
- Pakistan: 84%
- Bangladesh: 82%

Middle East / North Africa
- Iraq: 91%
- Palestinians: 89%
- Morocco: 83%
- Egypt: 74%
- Jordan: 71%
- Tunisia: 56%
- Lebanon: 29%

Sub-Saharan Africa
- Niger: 86%
- Djibouti: 82%
- DR Congo: 74%
- Nigeria: 71%
- Uganda: 66%
- Ethiopia: 65%
- Mozambique: 65%
- Kenya: 64%
- Mali: 63%
- Ghana: 58%
- Senegal: 55%
- Cameroon: 53%
- Liberia: 52%
- Chad: 47%
- Guinea Bissau: 47%
- Tanzania: 37%

Source: Pew Research Center, April 2013.

Nigeria, roughly half of the population is Christian and half is Muslim. In twelve of the Muslim-majority states, Sharia law has already been adopted. However, the federal government, which tends to be dominated by Christians, has at times overturned the rulings of Sharia courts.

Support for Sharia as the official law of the land also is widespread among Muslims in the Middle East and North Africa, especially in Iraq (91 percent) and the Palestinian territories (89 percent). Only in Lebanon does opinion lean in the opposite direction: 29 percent of Lebanese Muslims favor making Sharia the law of the land, while 66 percent oppose it. Again, this follows the historical trend—Lebanon was once considered to be among the most cosmopolitan of the Arab states. It also is home to a relatively large population of Christians, as well as to many Shia Muslims, who tend to have a different interpretation of Sharia from Sunni Muslims.

In the Central Asian states that once were part of the Soviet Union, as well as in southern and eastern Europe, support for Sharia is relatively weak. Fewer than half of Muslims in all the countries surveyed in these regions favor making sharia their country's official law. Support for Sharia as the law of the land is greatest among Russian Muslims, at 42 percent. In places like Kazakhstan and Azerbaijan, fewer than 10 percent of Muslims wanted to see the adoption of Sharia as the law of the land, according to the 2013 data.

Text-Dependent Questions

1. What is the day of congregational prayer for Muslims?
2. What are Islamists?

Research Project

Write a one-page description of the Holy Mosque of Mecca. When was it constructed? What is its size? How is it designed? What is the historical significance of Mecca to Muslims?

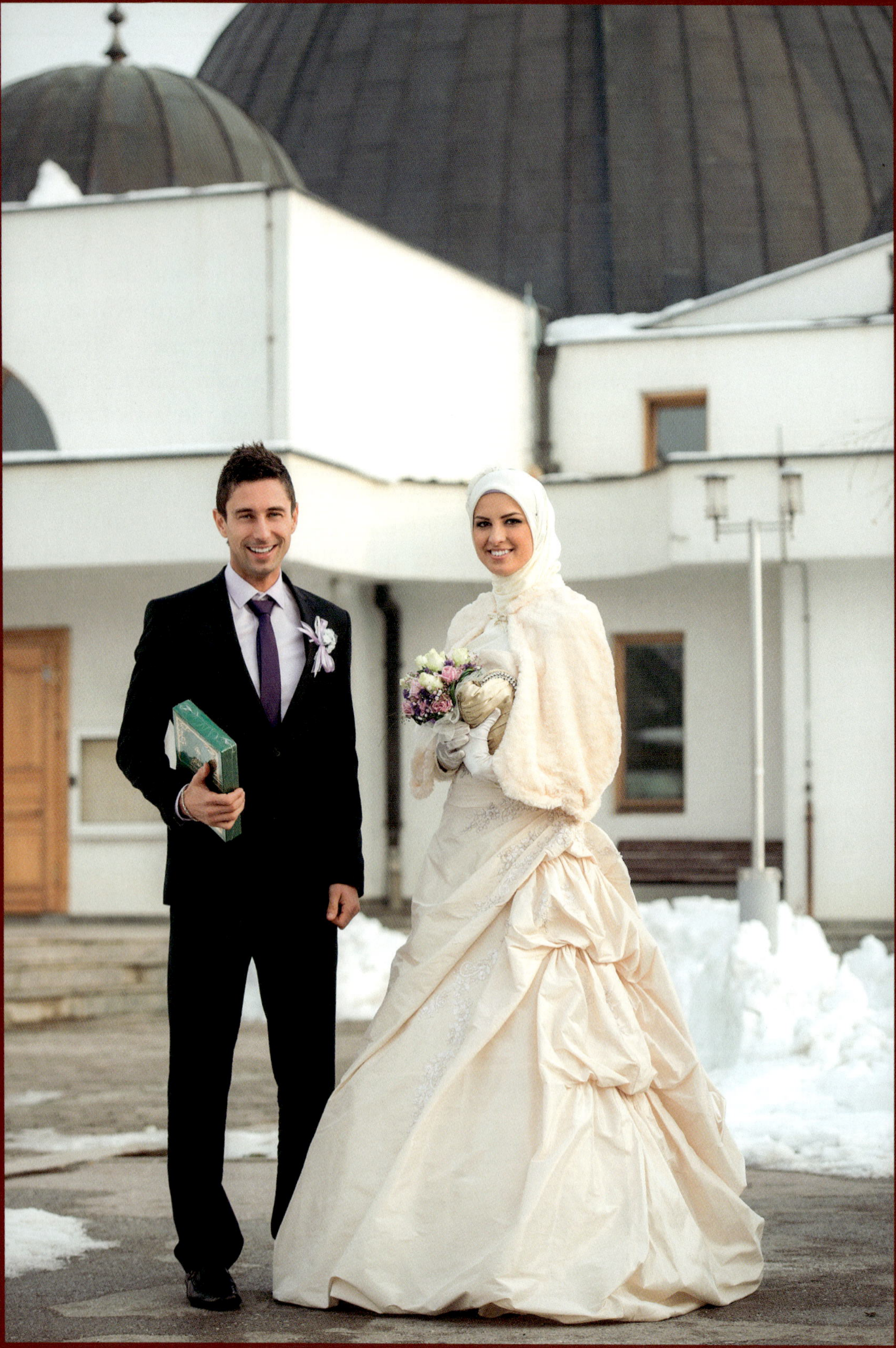

4

Views on Culture and Values

In its surveys of the Islamic world, the Pew Research Center has asked tens of thousands of Muslims for their opinions about a wide variety of cultural practices and values. The following provides an overview of cultural practices that are common in the Islamic world, and explains what the Pew, Gallup, and other organization have learned about the views of Muslims toward these practices.

Love and Marriage

Marriages are happy events for families in the Islamic world. Young Muslim men and women may choose to marry after meeting socially and falling in love, but the traditional arranged marriage, in which the parents choose who their children will marry, still occurs in some rural areas. Islamic law decrees the young couple must agree to the match.

Even when a young Muslim meets a potential marriage partner,

Opposite: A just-married bride and groom pose outside of a mosque. Social practices, such as the ceremonies surrounding weddings, vary widely throughout the Muslim world.

there are strict rules regulating the time they can spend together. Western-style dating is particularly rare in rural areas; instead, young single men and women often meet in a group setting, then ask their families to help them find out more about a person that interests them. In *cosmopolitan* urban centers, like Cairo, Damascus, or Beirut, men and women who are engaged will often go out together, although they are supposed to stay in public places in order to avoid the temptation of premarital sex. Nevertheless, like all societies in the world, premarital sex does take place, although it is not as common as in the West.

The Quran forbids sex outside of marriage, and a Pew Research Center survey from 2013 found that most Muslims have strong views against premarital sex, as well as extramarital sex. In twenty-nine of the thirty-six countries where the question was asked, more than 75 percent of respondents condemned premarital sex as being immoral. The highest percentages occurred in Thailand (99 percent), Jordan (96 percent), Lebanon (96 percent) and Egypt (95 percent).

Muslims in Southern and Eastern Europe, as well as in sub-Saharan Africa, were more tolerant of sex outside of marriage. Pew found that 26 percent of Muslims in Bosnia-Herzegovina and 25 percent of Muslims in Albania felt that sex outside of marriage was morally acceptable. Nearly two of every ten Muslims share this view in Guinea Bissau (19 percent), Chad (18 percent), and Uganda (18 percent), which are all located in sub-Saharan Africa.

Before a couple is married, the families of the bride and groom often negotiate a marriage contract that may include a payment of

Words to Understand in This Chapter

cosmopolitan—used to describe a tolerant place where many cultures and ideas can blend together.
polygamy—marriage in which a spouse of either sex may have more than one mate at the same time.

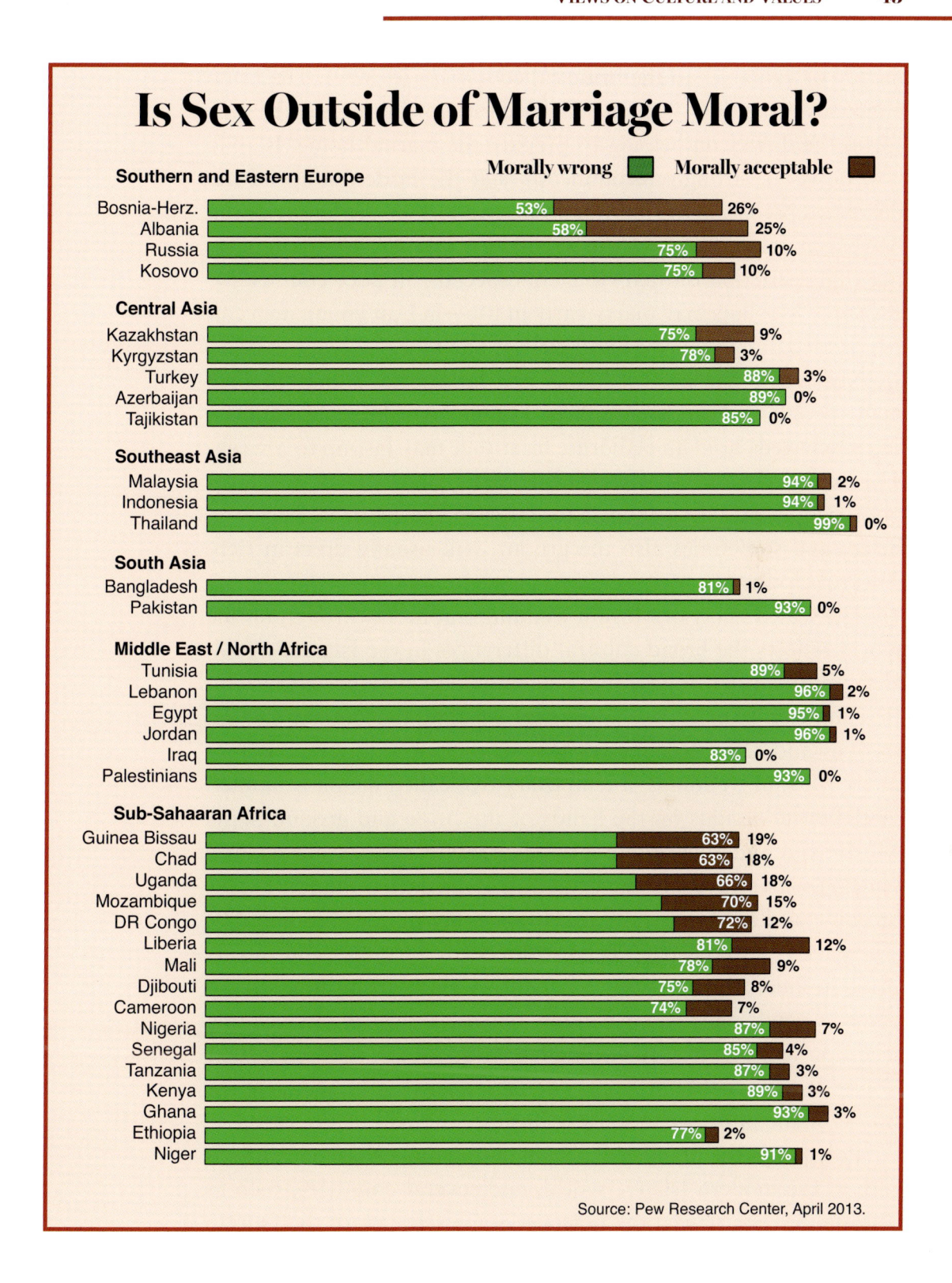

Is Sex Outside of Marriage Moral?

Morally wrong ▮ Morally acceptable ▮

Southern and Eastern Europe
Country	Morally wrong	Morally acceptable
Bosnia-Herz.	53%	26%
Albania	58%	25%
Russia	75%	10%
Kosovo	75%	10%

Central Asia
Country	Morally wrong	Morally acceptable
Kazakhstan	75%	9%
Kyrgyzstan	78%	3%
Turkey	88%	3%
Azerbaijan	89%	0%
Tajikistan	85%	0%

Southeast Asia
Country	Morally wrong	Morally acceptable
Malaysia	94%	2%
Indonesia	94%	1%
Thailand	99%	0%

South Asia
Country	Morally wrong	Morally acceptable
Bangladesh	81%	1%
Pakistan	93%	0%

Middle East / North Africa
Country	Morally wrong	Morally acceptable
Tunisia	89%	5%
Lebanon	96%	2%
Egypt	95%	1%
Jordan	96%	1%
Iraq	83%	0%
Palestinians	93%	0%

Sub-Sahaaran Africa
Country	Morally wrong	Morally acceptable
Guinea Bissau	63%	19%
Chad	63%	18%
Uganda	66%	18%
Mozambique	70%	15%
DR Congo	72%	12%
Liberia	81%	12%
Mali	78%	9%
Djibouti	75%	8%
Cameroon	74%	7%
Nigeria	87%	7%
Senegal	85%	4%
Tanzania	87%	3%
Kenya	89%	3%
Ghana	93%	3%
Ethiopia	77%	2%
Niger	91%	1%

Source: Pew Research Center, April 2013.

money or valuables to the bride called a *mahr* (dowry). The bride either saves the dowry as financial security for herself, or she may spend the dowry on helping to prepare the marital home. Islamic law, however, strongly recommends that the bride not spend the dowry on preparing the marital home and forbids the family of the bride from taking the dowry or spending it on themselves. (In practice this restriction is often violated, especially in poor countries.)

Some Muslims may marry early in life—in Iran young men can be married at age fourteen and girls at age nine.

Nearly all Muslim weddings are large affairs that involve many people and can last for days. In many Muslim communities, the newlyweds hold an elaborate feast that may last up to a week. The extended families of both bride and groom attend, and local poor people are often invited to share in the feast as well. The bride, and sometimes also the groom, will usually dress in rich, colorful clothes.

The wide variety of Muslim wedding traditions throughout the world reflects the broad cultural differences in the Islamic world. Celebrations often follow local customs that may predate Islam. In countries like Malaysia or Afghanistan, the couple sits on thrones and is treated like royalty on their wedding day. Before many Muslim weddings, a temporary dye called henna is painted in elaborate designs on the hands of the bride and groom. Some Muslims in Sudan celebrate a marriage with races, contests, and dancing with swords. In the United Arab Emirates, the bride stays at home and has no visitors for 40 days before the wedding day, when she is covered from head to toe with perfumes and oils. A bride in Palestine may wear a headdress made from hundreds of coins. A newly married husband in Yemen follows an old wedding tradition when he tries to step on his wife's foot as they enter their house. If he succeeds, it is considered a sign that he will rule the house. If she pulls her foot away in time, she will be the boss.

Polygamy (the practice of a man taking more than one wife) is rare in the modern Islamic world, and several countries, such as Tunisia, have outlawed the practice. Some scholars of the Qur'an

VIEWS ON CULTURE AND VALUES

View of the Jemaa el Fna Square in Marrakesh, Morocco.

have argued that the practice was accepted at the time of Muhammad's revelations because it was very widespread on the Arabian Peninsula, but they point out that the Qur'an treats the practice of polygamy with skepticism, if not outright hostility. In the Arab society of Muhammad's day, warriors often died young, leaving behind young widows who would not be cared for unless they remarried. Qur'an 4: 3 amended an existing custom that allowed men to take unlimited wives; Muslims were permitted four wives, but only if the man could afford to care for each of them equally. In the modern era, some Muslims have proposed that Qur'an 4: 129—which reads in part, "You are never able to be fair and just between women even if that were your ardent desire"—supports monogamy.

Today, Muslims in most parts of the world consider polygamy to be morally unacceptable. Muslims in Central Asia and Europe

Is Polygamy Moral?

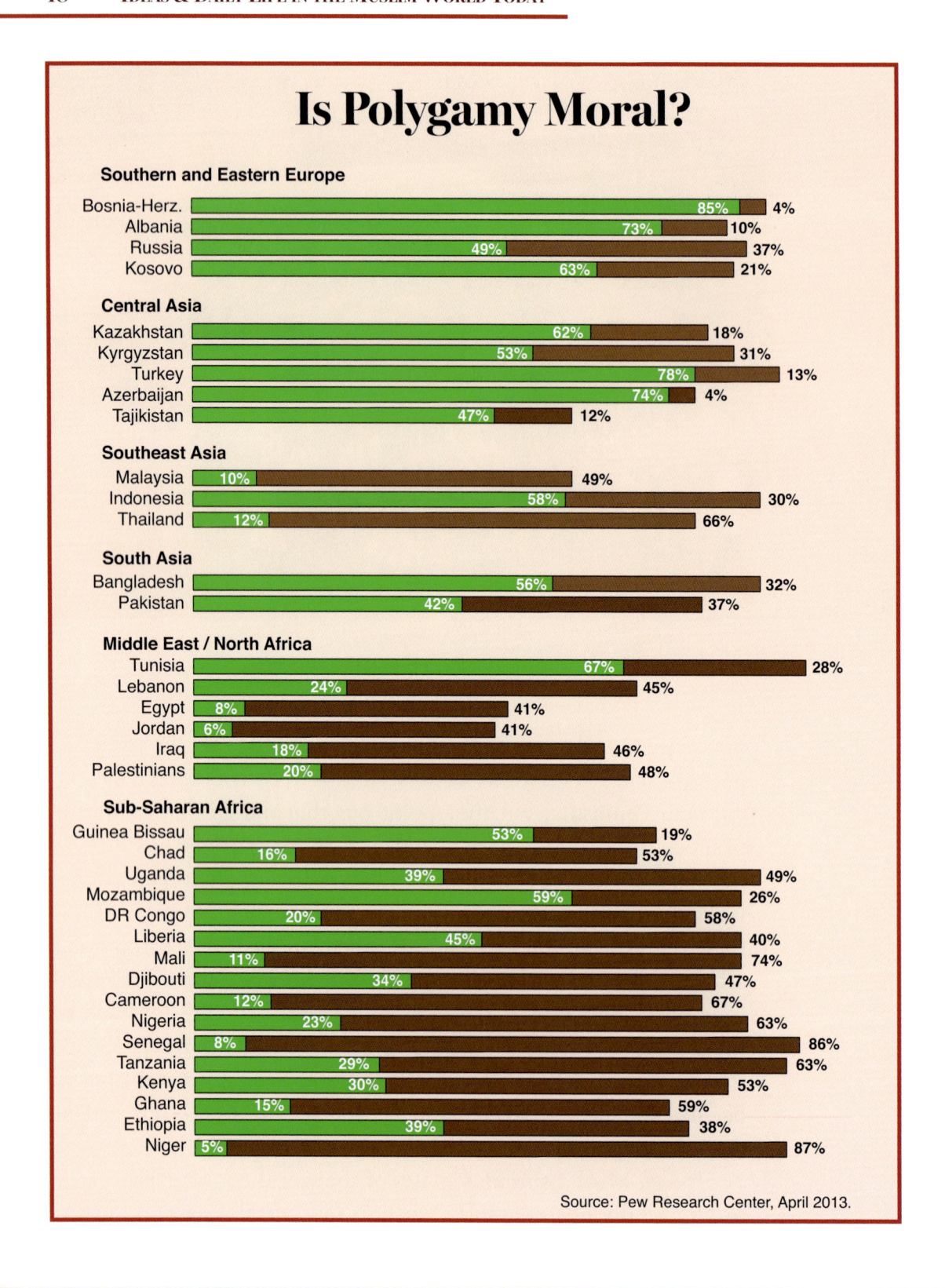

Southern and Eastern Europe

Country	Moral	Immoral
Bosnia-Herz.	85%	4%
Albania	73%	10%
Russia	49%	37%
Kosovo	63%	21%

Central Asia

Country	Moral	Immoral
Kazakhstan	62%	18%
Kyrgyzstan	53%	31%
Turkey	78%	13%
Azerbaijan	74%	4%
Tajikistan	47%	12%

Southeast Asia

Country	Moral	Immoral
Malaysia	10%	49%
Indonesia	58%	30%
Thailand	12%	66%

South Asia

Country	Moral	Immoral
Bangladesh	56%	32%
Pakistan	42%	37%

Middle East / North Africa

Country	Moral	Immoral
Tunisia	67%	28%
Lebanon	24%	45%
Egypt	8%	41%
Jordan	6%	41%
Iraq	18%	46%
Palestinians	20%	48%

Sub-Saharan Africa

Country	Moral	Immoral
Guinea Bissau	53%	19%
Chad	16%	53%
Uganda	39%	49%
Mozambique	59%	26%
DR Congo	20%	58%
Liberia	45%	40%
Mali	11%	74%
Djibouti	34%	47%
Cameroon	12%	67%
Nigeria	23%	63%
Senegal	8%	86%
Tanzania	29%	63%
Kenya	30%	53%
Ghana	15%	59%
Ethiopia	39%	38%
Niger	5%	87%

Source: Pew Research Center, April 2013.

are the most likely to say that polygamy is morally wrong. In most countries surveyed from these regions by Pew in 2013, more than 60 percent took this position. The highest opposition to polygamy was found in Bosnia (85 percent) and Turkey (78 percent); Russia (49 percent) and Tajikistan (47 percent) had the lowest opposition.

Acceptance of polygamy was considerably higher in sub-Saharan Africa. Pew found that more than 60 percent of Muslims felt that polygamy was acceptable in Niger (87 percent), Senegal (86 percent), Mali (74 percent), Cameroon (67 percent), Tanzania (63 percent), and Nigeria (63 percent).

In the Arab states of the Middle East and North Africa, more than four in ten Muslims told Pew that polygamy was morally acceptable in the Palestinian territories (48 percent), Iraq (46 percent) Lebanon (45 percent), Jordan (41 percent), and Egypt (41 percent). In the 2001 Gallup Poll of the Islamic World, a majority of those polled in Saudi Arabia, Kuwait, Jordan, and Lebanon said they did not support polygamy.

In many of the countries surveyed, Pew found that beliefs about the moral status of polygamy were strongly linked to support for Sharia as the official law of the land. Muslims who told Pew they wanted to live under Islamic law were consistently more likely to say polygamy is an acceptable practice than are those who did not want Sharia as official law.

Raising a Family

The married couple will soon turn to having children. Islamic law permits them to use birth control to limit the number of children they have. However, a large family is valued in many Muslim societies.

A newborn baby quickly receives an initiation into Islam. As soon as the umbilical cord is cut, many Muslims follow a tradition of whispering the Muslim call to prayer—the same words the child will hear from the local mosque five times each day—in each ear. Other parents whisper other things, such as the first chapter of the

Qur'an. To give thanks for the birth, the parents may also follow an old Arab custom of shaving the baby's head and giving the poor an amount of gold or silver equal to the weight of the hair. A sheep or other animal is sometimes slaughtered and eaten in celebration of the birth.

The parents name the baby between seven and forty days after birth in a ceremony with relatives and friends. Islamic law provides guidelines for parents in choosing names, which all have meanings. A name may describe a positive quality about the child, or express the wishes of the parent for the child. Parents may also name their children after Muhammad or other prophets or heroes of Islamic history. The name cannot be tasteless, offensive, or indicate that the child serves anyone other than Allah. Some common Arabic names for boys include "Abd Allah" ("servant of Allah"), "Ali" ("excellent"), and "Karim" ("generous"). Some popular girls' names include "Fatima" (this was the name of a daughter of Muhammad), "Nawal" ("gift"), and "Iman" ("faith").

A child born to Muslim parents will learn about his or her religion on a daily basis. Among the first words taught to many children are, "In the name of Allah, the Merciful, the Compassionate." With these words, Muslims affirm their connection to Allah in their daily lives. Children see their parents praying and join in the prayers after learning how they are performed. Parents are responsible for ensuring that their children understand their religion, in addition to teaching them manners and proper behavior.

Islam places a high value on children respecting their parents and honoring them by growing up to be honest and decent adults. Muslim children are taught to speak politely to their elders and help with household chores or duties. In some cultures children are expected to stand when their parents enter a room.

In the Islamic world, when a person reaches puberty he or she is considered an adult. Adulthood brings additional responsibilities for proper behavior, and the young adults are held accountable for their actions. Adult Muslims are expected to care for aging parents. Even after a parents' death, some Muslims may feel an obligation to fulfill promises their parents made. They may even go on the *hajj* to Mecca for their mother or father if either parent did not go before dying.

According to the Gallup poll of the Islamic world, many Muslims felt that honesty and tolerance are the two most important qualities they can teach their children at home. When given a list of seven qualities—honesty, tolerance, obedience, independence, perseverance, leadership, and imagination—and asked which three were the most important, between 82 percent and 92 percent of people in Lebanon, Kuwait, Saudi Arabia, Jordan, Turkey, Pakistan, and Iran selected honesty. Tolerance was chosen by between 60 percent and 86 percent of people in those seven countries plus Morocco. (The question was not asked in Indonesia.)

Perseverance and independence seemed to be valued about the same. Between 24 and 47 percent of the people in the eight coun-

Muslim children are taught about their religion from an early age.

tries where the question was asked selected independence as an important quality, compared to a range of 23 to 57 percent for perseverance. Leadership and imagination were the least valued qualities. The most controversial quality was obedience, as the percentage of people who listed it in the top three ranged from 71 percent in Pakistan to 21 percent in Iran.

The Gallup Organization found that the importance of obedience was closely related to the respondents' levels of education. In all of the countries surveyed, people with higher education (secondary school or higher) were much less likely to rate obedience among the top three qualities than were people with a lower education (up to elementary school). The difference of opinion between the two educational groups was greater than 20 percentage points in Kuwait, Jordan, Pakistan, Morocco, and Turkey, and between 10 and 15 percentage points in Saudi Arabia, Lebanon, and Iran.

Education in the Islamic World

Depending on where a child lives, he or she may attend a public school or an Islamic school, called a madrasa. In many countries, religious education is the core of learning. Boys and girls learn about the Qur'an even before they can read it. After Muslims learn to read, many will work for years to memorize the entire Qur'an. Because Muslims believe that the Qur'an can only be understood in Arabic, children who speak another language often learn Arabic in addition to their native language. When the child memorizes the entire Qur'an, the family may mark the event by inviting relatives and friends to a celebration, where the child will recite passages from memory. In their schools young Muslims also study the same subjects American students do—mathematics, science, history, art, and so on.

In the nine countries of the Islamic world surveyed by the Gallup Organization, levels of education vary greatly. Kuwait has the highest number of people achieving a secondary level of edu-

Indonesian girls work on their lessons in a school on the island of Java. The Gallup Organization has found that Indonesia has one of the best educational systems in the Muslim world.

cation, at 81 percent, followed by Saudi Arabia (74 percent), Indonesia (72 percent), and Jordan (67 percent). The lowest-ranking countries are Pakistan (12 percent) and Morocco (20 percent). In Pakistan, 36 percent of the population receives no formal education at all, followed by Morocco at 26 percent.

In the urban centers of the Islamic world, college education is becoming more common. In many Muslim countries colleges are free and public, so even in rural areas an increasing number of Muslims end up going to college. According to the Gallup Poll, among the nine countries studied Kuwait has the greatest percentage of people who complete studies at a college or university (28 percent), followed by Saudi Arabia and Lebanon (each at 18 percent). By comparison, data from the 2000 US Census indicates that 15.5 percent of Americans had completed a college degree.

In many Islamic countries, men and women have equal opportunities to receive an education. In Kuwait, for example, 81 percent of men and 80 percent of women have completed a secondary level of education, while in Saudi Arabia the figures are 76 percent of men and 71 percent of women. Of the countries included in the Gallup Organization's survey, Turkey had the largest "gender gap" when it came to education (54 percent of men had completed at least a secondary level of education, compared to 31 percent of women). Women have great opportunities to receive an education in many other Islamic countries as well. Females make up 52 percent of the medical students in Egypt, and can be found in colleges and universities throughout the Islamic world.

The Gallup Organization also found that in the countries with the lowest educational levels, there are wide gaps between the percentages of men and women who receive no formal education. In Morocco, 41 percent of women report that they have not received any schooling, compared to 11 percent of men. The situation is similar in Pakistan, where 49 percent of women have no education, compared to 22 percent of men.

Divorce in Islamic Society

Divorce (*talaq*) is not taken lightly in Islamic law. In pre-Islamic Arabia men could divorce their wives at will, but in Islamic law a husband must declare his intention to divorce his wife three times to make it irrevocable. Qur'an 4: 35 first counsels arbitration when divorce is discussed. If this fails, the advisable course is for the husband to say "I divorce you" once and enter a three-month waiting period to see if the couple can reconcile and to make sure the wife is not pregnant. If the husband reconsiders, the couple can get back together. If they do not reconcile, and the husband utters the divorce declaration twice more, their divorce is final. In another approach, the husband makes the

Attitudes Toward Divorce

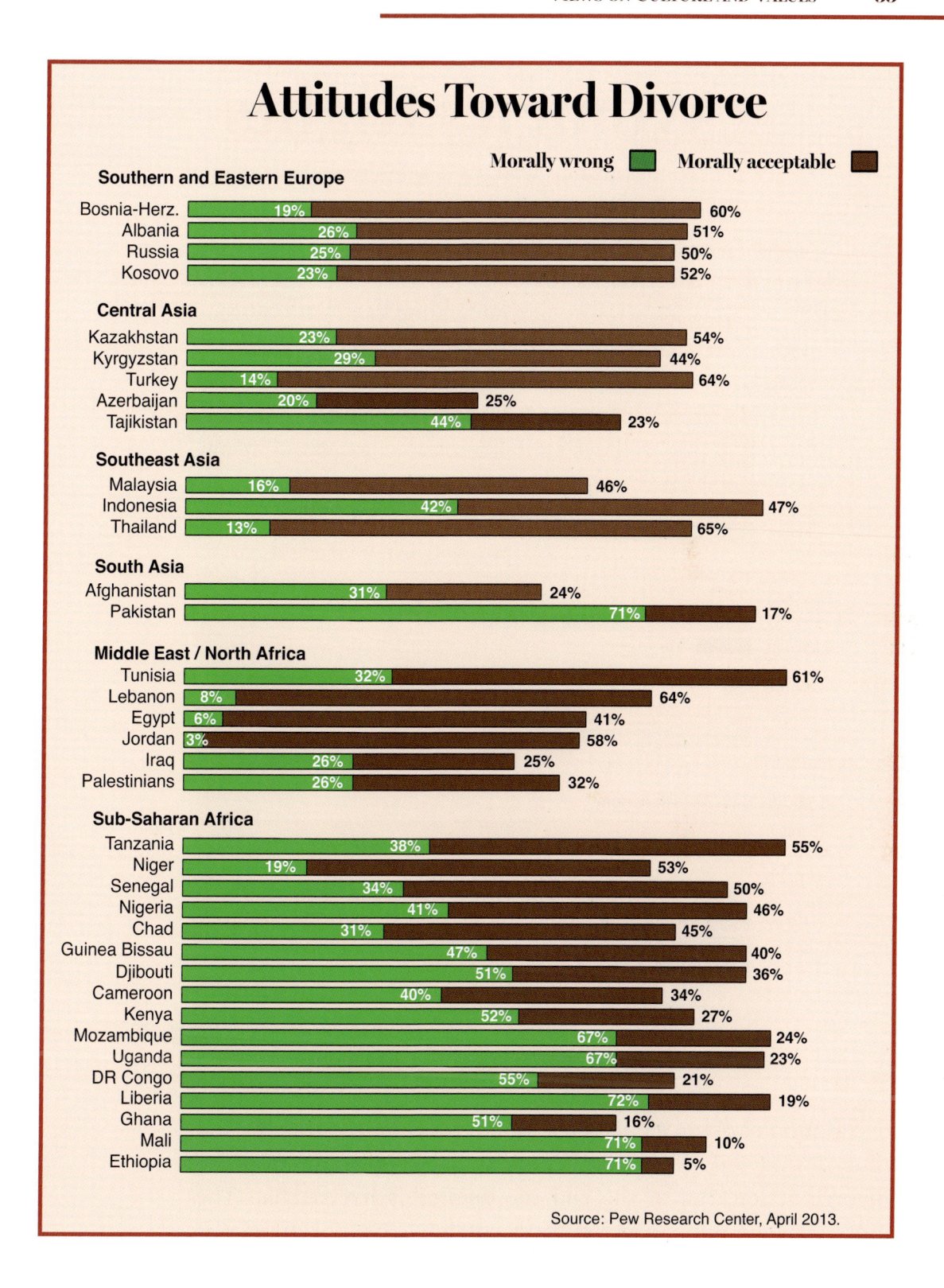

Morally wrong (green) · **Morally acceptable** (brown)

Southern and Eastern Europe
Country	Morally wrong	Morally acceptable
Bosnia-Herz.	19%	60%
Albania	26%	51%
Russia	25%	50%
Kosovo	23%	52%

Central Asia
Country	Morally wrong	Morally acceptable
Kazakhstan	23%	54%
Kyrgyzstan	29%	44%
Turkey	14%	64%
Azerbaijan	20%	25%
Tajikistan	44%	23%

Southeast Asia
Country	Morally wrong	Morally acceptable
Malaysia	16%	46%
Indonesia	42%	47%
Thailand	13%	65%

South Asia
Country	Morally wrong	Morally acceptable
Afghanistan	31%	24%
Pakistan	71%	17%

Middle East / North Africa
Country	Morally wrong	Morally acceptable
Tunisia	32%	61%
Lebanon	8%	64%
Egypt	6%	41%
Jordan	3%	58%
Iraq	26%	25%
Palestinians	26%	32%

Sub-Saharan Africa
Country	Morally wrong	Morally acceptable
Tanzania	38%	55%
Niger	19%	53%
Senegal	34%	50%
Nigeria	41%	46%
Chad	31%	45%
Guinea Bissau	47%	40%
Djibouti	51%	36%
Cameroon	40%	34%
Kenya	52%	27%
Mozambique	67%	24%
Uganda	67%	23%
DR Congo	55%	21%
Liberia	72%	19%
Ghana	51%	16%
Mali	71%	10%
Ethiopia	71%	5%

Source: Pew Research Center, April 2013.

Women's Rights

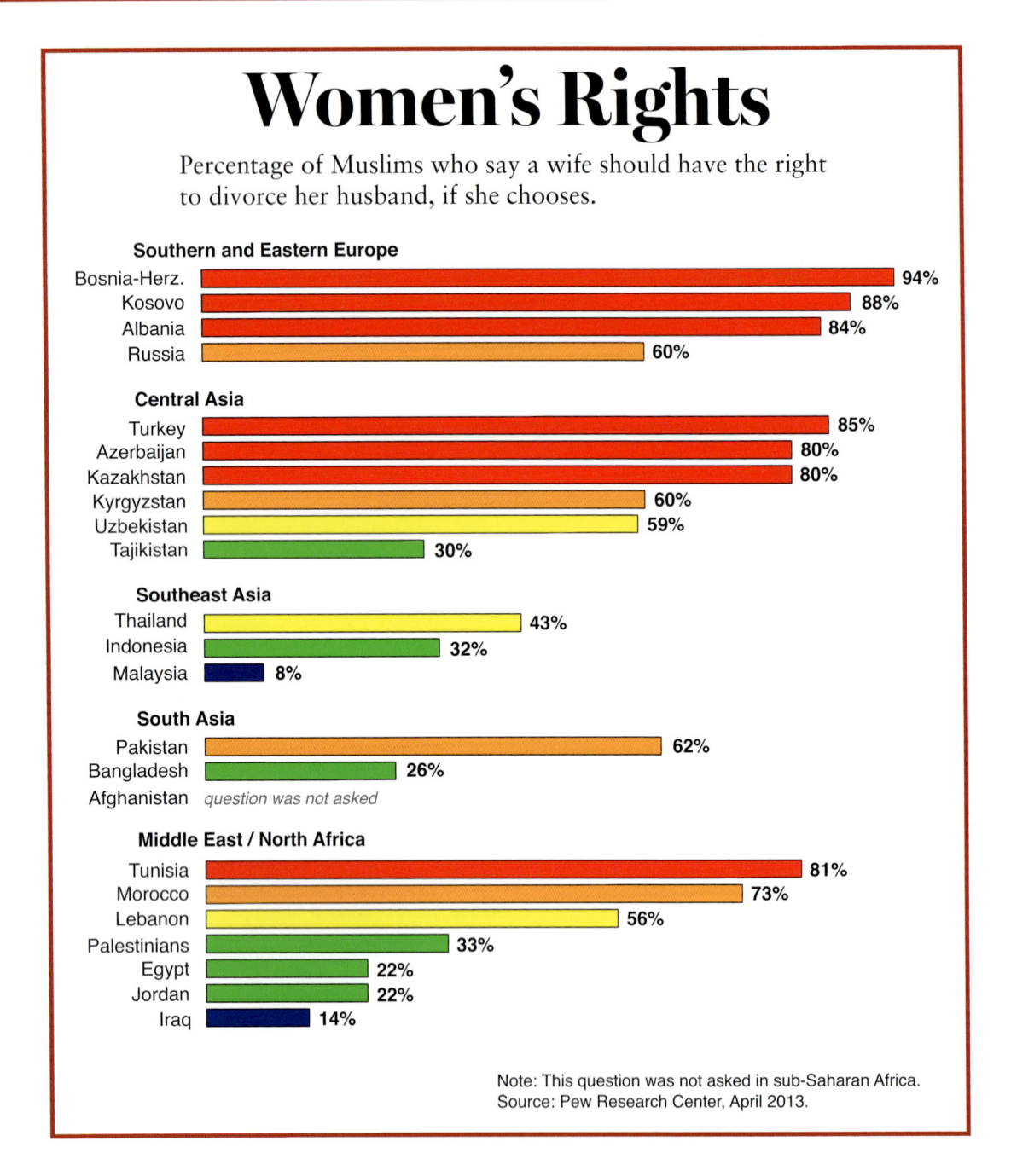

Percentage of Muslims who say a wife should have the right to divorce her husband, if she chooses.

Southern and Eastern Europe
- Bosnia-Herz.: 94%
- Kosovo: 88%
- Albania: 84%
- Russia: 60%

Central Asia
- Turkey: 85%
- Azerbaijan: 80%
- Kazakhstan: 80%
- Kyrgyzstan: 60%
- Uzbekistan: 59%
- Tajikistan: 30%

Southeast Asia
- Thailand: 43%
- Indonesia: 32%
- Malaysia: 8%

South Asia
- Pakistan: 62%
- Bangladesh: 26%
- Afghanistan: question was not asked

Middle East / North Africa
- Tunisia: 81%
- Morocco: 73%
- Lebanon: 56%
- Palestinians: 33%
- Egypt: 22%
- Jordan: 22%
- Iraq: 14%

Note: This question was not asked in sub-Saharan Africa.
Source: Pew Research Center, April 2013.

declaration of divorce once each month for three months. At any time during this three-month period, the couple can stop the divorce action, but at the end the divorce is irrevocable. The most frowned upon, and yet most common, type of divorce is the triple *talaq*, in which the husband utters the divorce formula three times all at once.

Women can sue for divorce only on limited grounds, such as the impotence or insanity of her husband or for desertion or failure to support. Quite often, however, women do not exercise their right to divorce because, in many male-dominated societies, they are not informed about their legal rights. In recent years some Muslim countries have expanded their laws to give women more grounds for divorce and to provide women with more material compensation when their husbands divorce them. However, in other Muslim countries such as Pakistan, Nigeria, and Saudi Arabia, women are not treated fairly by matrimonial or criminal courts. This does not change the fact that doctrinally Islamic law is clear in its opposition to discrimination against women.

Wife beating occurs in some parts of the Islamic world, but it is not looked upon favorably. Many Muslim countries criminalize the behavior, and a husband can go to prison for a period ranging from six months to three years for assaulting his wife. Such prosecutions are common, especially in situations where there is a physical injury. In addition, one of the Hadith says, "The worst of men are those who beat their wives. [By doing so] they are no longer one of us." If wife beating occurs, neighbors and family usually intervene to stop the abuse, often reminding the offending husband of what the Prophet said about wife-beaters.

In recent years, the practice of stipulated divorces (known as *talaq al-tafwid*) has become more popular. The Prophet Muhammad sanctioned this practice during the early years of Islam, but there was much culture-based resistance. In these cases, a stipulation is entered into the marital contract dictating that if the husband commits certain conduct, the wife acquires an immediate right to a divorce. In effect, the stipulation acts as a prenuptial agreement that grants women considerable power within a marriage by challenging the traditionally exclusive male prerogative over divorce. In the modern age, a large number of women rekindled this practice by entering into prenuptial agree-

Women's Rights

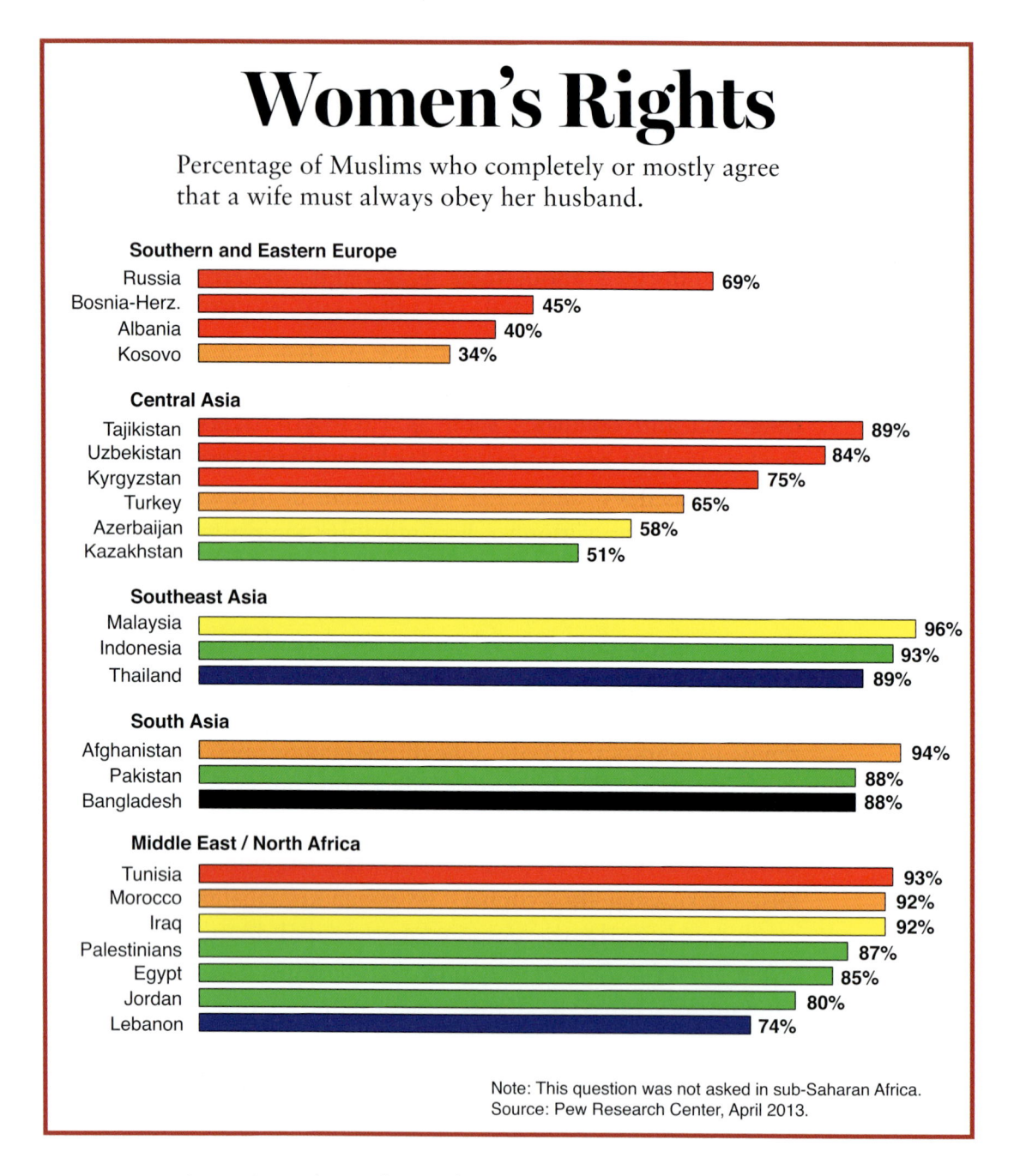

Percentage of Muslims who completely or mostly agree that a wife must always obey her husband.

Southern and Eastern Europe
- Russia: 69%
- Bosnia-Herz.: 45%
- Albania: 40%
- Kosovo: 34%

Central Asia
- Tajikistan: 89%
- Uzbekistan: 84%
- Kyrgyzstan: 75%
- Turkey: 65%
- Azerbaijan: 58%
- Kazakhstan: 51%

Southeast Asia
- Malaysia: 96%
- Indonesia: 93%
- Thailand: 89%

South Asia
- Afghanistan: 94%
- Pakistan: 88%
- Bangladesh: 88%

Middle East / North Africa
- Tunisia: 93%
- Morocco: 92%
- Iraq: 92%
- Palestinians: 87%
- Egypt: 85%
- Jordan: 80%
- Lebanon: 74%

Note: This question was not asked in sub-Saharan Africa.
Source: Pew Research Center, April 2013.

ments granting wives the right to divorce their husbands, if the wives wish to do so.

When divorce occurs, children enter the custody of either the mother or the father depending on their age. In most instances, boys under the age of nine and girls under the age of 12 are given into the custody of the mother. Thereafter, custody reverts to the father.

In 2013, the Pew Research Center asked Muslims in thirty-seven countries about their opinions on the morality of divorce. In fifteen of those countries, at least half of Muslims considered divorce a morally acceptable practice. The highest rates of acceptance were in Thailand (65 percent), Turkey (64 percent), Lebanon (64 percent), Bangladesh (62 percent), Tunisia (61 percent), and Bosnia-Herzegovina (60 percent).

In ten countries, at least half of the Muslims believed divorce is morally wrong, with more than seven out of ten people opposed to divorce in Liberia (72 percent), Mali (71 percent), Ethiopia (71 percent) and Pakistan (71 percent).

In most countries, at least 20 percent of Muslims said that divorce is not a moral issue or that it depends on the situation. In general, younger Muslims tended to be more likely to say that divorce was morally acceptable, and men were somewhat more likely than women to say that divorce is morally acceptable.

Text-Dependent Questions

1. How to Muslims in sub-Saharan Africa tend to feel about polygamy?
2. What are the two most important qualities that Muslims want to teach their children at home, according to the Gallup Organization's polling data?

Research Project

Two of the most important religious holidays in Islam are Eid al-Fitr, which occurs at the end of the sacred month of Ramadan, and Eid al-Adha, the last day of the hajj period. Choose one of these festivals, and do some research to find out more about why that particular festival is important to Muslims, how it is traditionally celebrated, and whether Syrians celebrate the festival differently than Muslims in other countries. Write a two-page report on the festival.

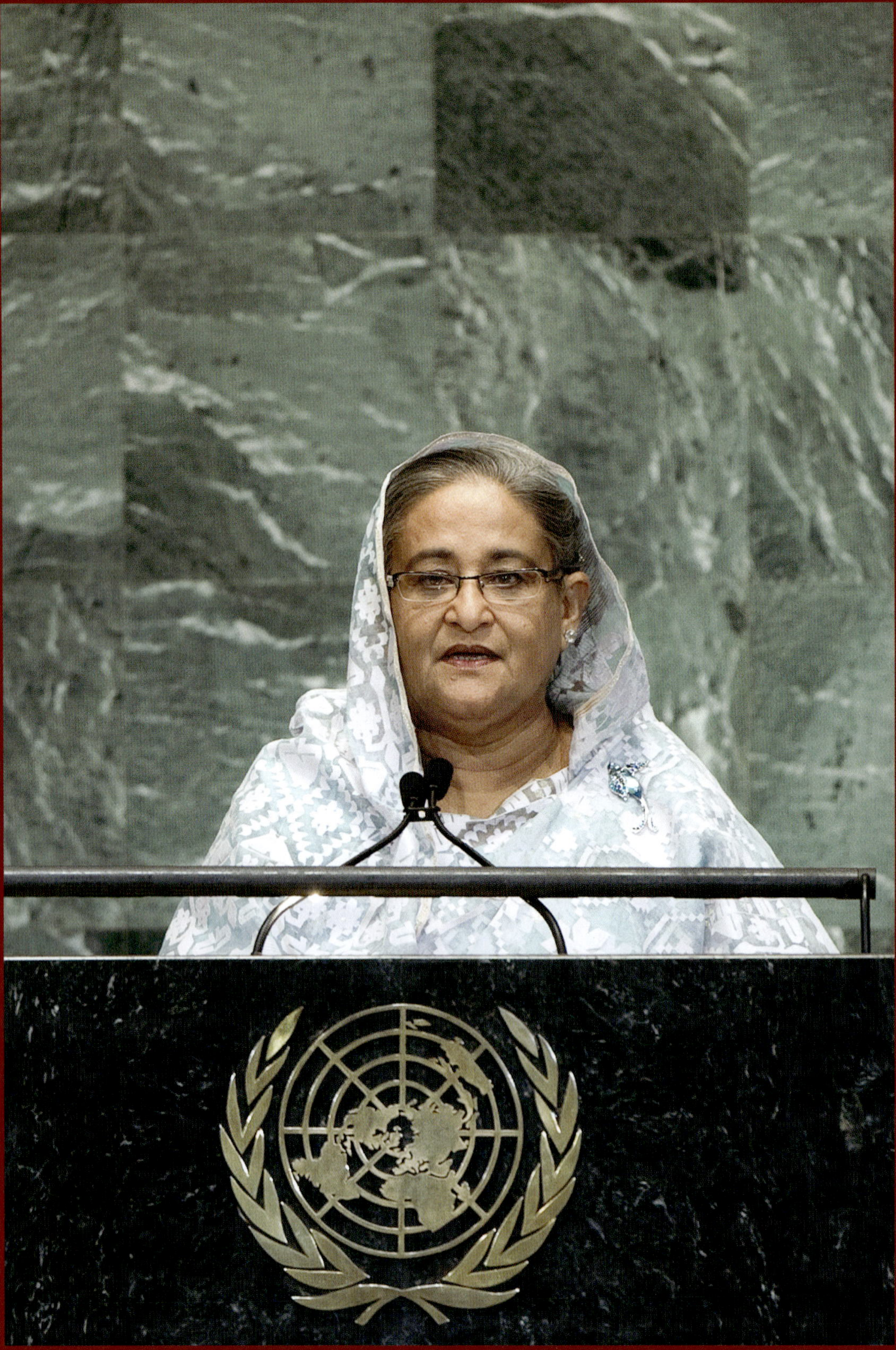

5

Women and Islam

Many westerners believe that the role of women in Muslim societies is one of the biggest differences between the Islamic world and the West. Images of Muslim women veiled from head to toe and stories about the persecution of women in the Islamic world circulate throughout the United States and other western countries. However, the status of women in Islamic countries is more complicated than the pictures and *stereotypes* common in the Western media. For example, no woman has ever been elected president or vice-president of the United States, but in 1989 a woman named Benazir Bhutto became the leader of Pakistan. Since then Turkey, Bangladesh, Indonesia, Senegal, Kyrgyzstan, and Kosovo have also chosen Muslim women as national leaders. Even in Iran, where a strict version of Islamic law is enforced, women can get jobs, go to college, run businesses, and vote in national elections. Egyptian women began a women's liberation movement at the beginning of the

Opposite: Sheikh Hasina, prime minister of Bangladesh, addresses the United Nations. The role of women in Islamic countries varies widely. In some places, such as Bangladesh and Pakistan, women are fully involved in politics and public life. Other countries, such as Saudi Arabia, place greater restrictions on the role of women.

20th century, before a similar movement emerged in the United States.

Although some people in the West condemn treatment of women in the Islamic world as unfair, westerners often forget that their own societies did not give women equal treatment until very recently. Before laws and attitudes changed during the 1960s and 1970s, women in the United States were commonly excluded from the best colleges and the best jobs, earned less pay than men for doing the same jobs, and had fewer rights to own property or borrow money. There are still Americans alive today who can remember when women were not allowed to vote—a right they won in 1920.

Islam's Treatment of Women

Before the rise of Islam, women living on the Arabian Peninsula had few rights. The Arab societies of Muhammad's time were patriarchal, and men were the leaders of families and tribes. Women could not inherit money or property, and widows were considered the property of their deceased husband's family. *Polygyny*, or the practice of having multiple wives, was widespread, and men could marry or divorce at will.

It is important to keep in mind, however, that in most ancient societies women had few or no rights. In the Indus Valley civilizations, and in the ancient Greek and Roman empires, women were often considered to be possessions of their husbands. Women were even treated differently from men in the writings and teachings of early Jewish and Christian leaders.

Words to Understand in This Chapter

polygyny—the practice of having more than one wife or female mate at one time.
stereotype—a widely held, but oversimplified, image or idea of a particular type of person or thing.

Atifete Jahjaga, the current president of the predominantly Muslim country of Kosovo in eastern Europe, was elected in 2011.

Islam improved the status of women. The Prophet Muhammad taught that women had legal rights equal to those of men. The Qur'an gives women certain rights in marriage—they are no longer to be considered the property of their husbands—and says mothers deserve more respect from children than fathers do. Although Islamic law considers the most important duty of women to be their roles as wives, mothers, and homemakers, women are permitted to inherit property, manage their own money, and seek employment or own businesses. The Qur'an says that Muslims have a sacred duty to educate girls. Women participate in the religious duties of Islam, and can serve as religious leaders for other women. Muhammad expected women to fulfill different roles than men, but not necessarily unequal roles. In his final sermon the Prophet told his followers, "Treat your women well and be kind to them for they are your partners and committed helpers."

Before Muhammad's time, inheritance was passed only to men. The nearest male relative of the deceased received the inheritance, even if a female relative was more closely related. The fourth *sura* of the Qur'an granted women the right to inherit property. The Qur'an stipulates that wives, daughters, sisters, and mothers of the deceased are entitled to their share of the inheritance before the remainder is passed on the nearest male relative. In most cases, however, men were given twice the inheritance of women, the reasoning being that they were expected to bear financial responsibility for every member of their households.

Today, the treatment of women in the Islamic world varies from country to country, and depends as much on local customs and traditions as on religious views. In Turkey, Malaysia, and Indonesia, women have the same rights as men. Countries like Egypt have made steady advances in their treatment of women, and today women throughout the Islamic world have better access to education, health care, and jobs. At the other extreme, Saudi Arabia places some of the most severe restrictions on women. Women are banned from working in many professions, or even driving cars. They must get permission from their husband or father to do many other things, such as travel. Punishment for breaking the rules can be severe. And all women in Saudi Arabia—even non-Muslims—must veil themselves in public.

The Segregation of Women

In some Islamic societies, the veil is a powerful symbol of submission to Allah. Many Muslim women believe that to fulfill the Qur'an's requirement to dress modestly, they should cover their hair or even their entire face. Others veil themselves because it is the custom of their family or community. In Turkey, it is estimated that three-fourths of women wear the *hijab*, a head scarf that covers the hair and neck but leaves the face visible.

The veil is meant to protect women from unwanted attention

A Muslim woman walks down a street in Marseille, France, wearing the head covering known as a *hijab*. This photo was taken in 2008; since 2011, it has been illegal in France to wear such garments in public places.

from men, and some women want this protection. To many Muslim women, covering their hair and dressing modestly is a way to keep others from judging them by their appearance. A woman may also want to protect herself from the sun and dust—which is why men in some hot, dry regions wear a veil too.

In recent decades, women have donned veils to call for a return to Islamic values, or to protest against Western influence or corruption in their governments. Though veiling had been declining for some time in countries like Iraq, Syria, Lebanon, and Jordan, the practice has increased again. Ironically, as women are granted new freedoms to work and attend universities, the veil provides them with some protection from male harassment.

Some sociologists and anthropologists have argued that the practice of wearing a veil has become a means of expressing dissent and opposition to secular governments in the Islamic world, and to

Women's Rights

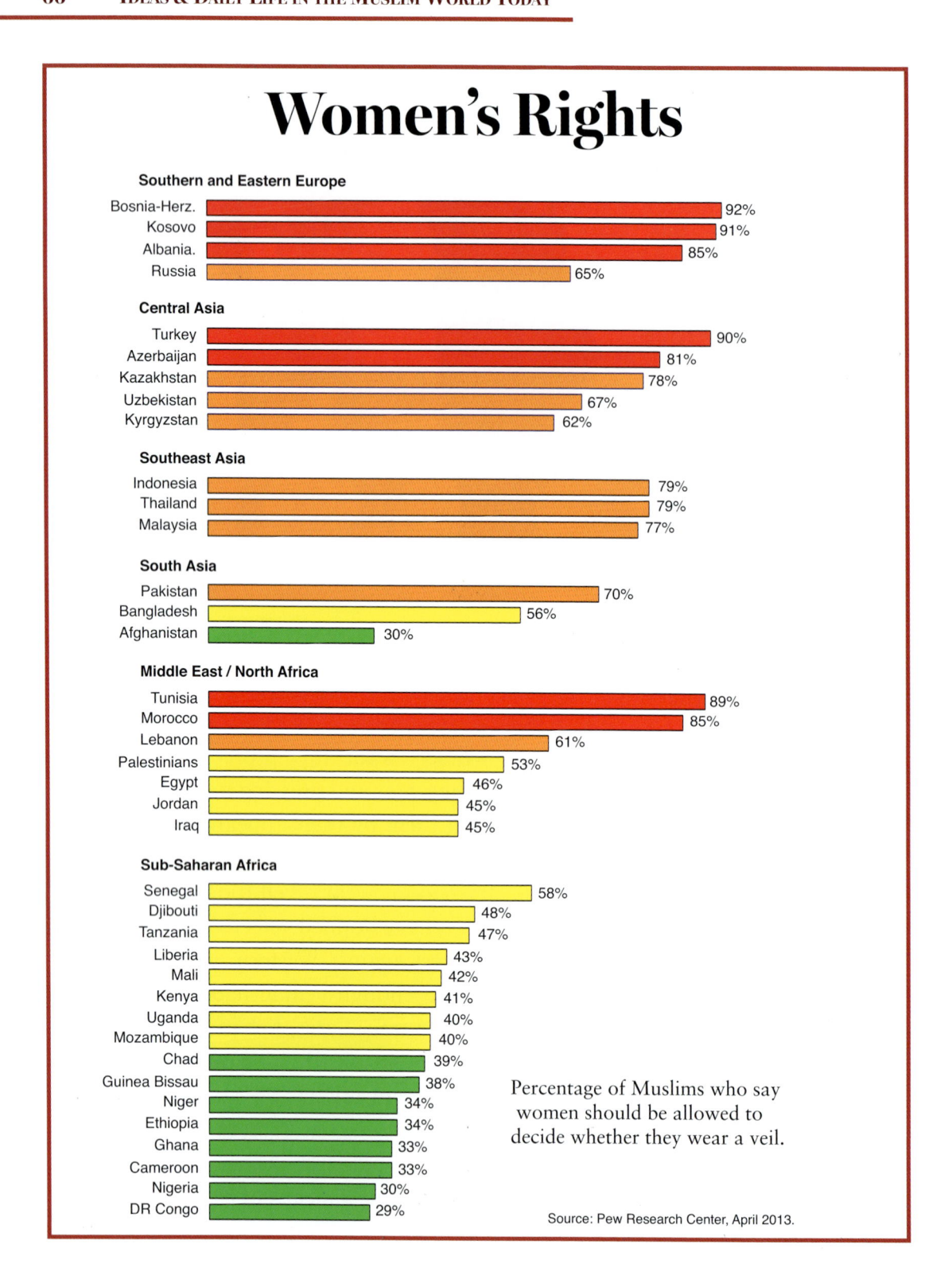

Southern and Eastern Europe
- Bosnia-Herz. 92%
- Kosovo 91%
- Albania. 85%
- Russia 65%

Central Asia
- Turkey 90%
- Azerbaijan 81%
- Kazakhstan 78%
- Uzbekistan 67%
- Kyrgyzstan 62%

Southeast Asia
- Indonesia 79%
- Thailand 79%
- Malaysia 77%

South Asia
- Pakistan 70%
- Bangladesh 56%
- Afghanistan 30%

Middle East / North Africa
- Tunisia 89%
- Morocco 85%
- Lebanon 61%
- Palestinians 53%
- Egypt 46%
- Jordan 45%
- Iraq 45%

Sub-Saharan Africa
- Senegal 58%
- Djibouti 48%
- Tanzania 47%
- Liberia 43%
- Mali 42%
- Kenya 41%
- Uganda 40%
- Mozambique 40%
- Chad 39%
- Guinea Bissau 38%
- Niger 34%
- Ethiopia 34%
- Ghana 33%
- Cameroon 33%
- Nigeria 30%
- DR Congo 29%

Percentage of Muslims who say women should be allowed to decide whether they wear a veil.

Source: Pew Research Center, April 2013.

social pressures that demand greater levels of Westernization and that dilute the people's sense of an Islamic identity. By wearing a veil, these experts say, women reassert their Islamic identity in response to the strong forces of Westernization.

Women who live in countries like Iran and Saudi Arabia have no choice but to veil themselves. Women forced to wear a *burqa* or *abaya*—garments that cover the head and entire body like a cape—suffer from the heat and inconvenience these types of garments cause. Women in such countries may face punishment from the authorities if they appear in public without the proper covering. However, the number of women forced to wear such garments are the minority in the Islamic world. Most Muslim women in Turkey, Lebanon, Tunisia, Morocco, Algeria, the former Soviet republics, and other Islamic countries wear either a simple scarf or no head covering at all.

The veil is one way that women may be segregated, or kept separate from men. In regions where women are required to cover themselves, they may also be restricted to separate areas in schools, restaurants, theatres, swimming pools, or gymnasiums. In places where rigid versions of Islam are enforced, women might have to visit certain public places only at special times, or may be banned from them altogether.

The Urdu word *purdah* ("seclusion") is equivalent to the Arabic word *hijab*. It broadly refers to the practice of secluding women in public through the various types of veiling. *Purdah* also refers more specifically to segregating the sexes by keeping women in seclusion at home behind a high wall, curtain, or screen. The latter type of seclusion is not practiced by many Muslims, but is particularly prevalent in India (where some Hindus also follow this practice).

In 2013, the Pew Research Center surveyed Muslims in thirty-nine countries to ask their opinion about women's rights. Pew found that in most of the countries surveyed, Muslims generally favored a woman's right to decide for herself whether to wear a veil in public. This view was especially prevalent in Europe, Central Asia, and Southeast Asia, and was held by more than nine out of ten Muslims in Bosnia-Herzegovina (92 percent), Kosovo (91 percent), and Turkey (90 percent).

There is less agreement among Muslims in the Middle East, North Africa, and South Asia. The North African states of Tunisia and Morocco tended to be more liberal in this regard, with 89 percent of Tunisians and 85 percent of Moroccans saying that women should have the right to choose whether they wear a veil. However, fewer than half of those surveyed in Egypt (46 percent), Jordan (45 percent), Iraq (45 percent), and Afghanistan (30 percent) felt the same way.

In sub-Saharan Africa, most Muslims believed women should be required to wear a veil. The only country in this region where a majority supported a woman's right to decide for herself was Senegal, where 58 percent supported the woman's right to choose. Fewer than one-third of Muslims supported allowing women this right in Nigeria and the Democratic Republic of the Congo.

Repression and Tradition

Although Islamic law gives specific freedoms to Muslim women, some Islamic countries have passed laws that place tight restrictions on the behavior and activities of women, above and beyond what is required by Islam.

In some parts of Africa, young women may undergo a barbaric procedure known as female circumcision or female genital mutilation (FGM). This horrible practice involves cutting off parts of the genitals of young girls. Although this practice is associated with the Islamic world, it is not derived from Islam; FGM occurs mostly in African communities, including non-Muslim areas. FGM is not mentioned in Islamic law, and most Muslim authorities say it is forbidden. Still, tens of thousands of African girls undergo this cruel practice, usually without benefit of painkillers or clean instruments. Today many activists and international human-rights organizations are working to stamp out this practice.

Many westerners feel that Islamic countries should not tolerate repressive attitudes and traditions concerning women. "The way Islam has been practiced in most Muslim societies for centuries has left millions of Muslim women with battered, bodies, minds, and souls," wrote Riffat Hassan, a religion professor in the United States, in a *Time* magazine article.

Throughout the Islamic world women's rights activists are claiming new freedom and power in many countries, but their progress is slow. Reformers often face stiff resistance from conservative people in their country who have a strict view of Islam or fear that changes for women will lead to unstable families or changes in other laws. Nevertheless, there have been many improvements in recent years. Bangladesh has increased the penalties for crimes against women, such as kidnapping and rape. Egypt has improved its divorce laws to help women; the government has also banned the practice of female circumcision. Morocco's legislature has set aside thirty seats for women. Women are permitted to vote and to run for election in many of the Arab Gulf states, such as Oman, Qatar, and Bahrain, just as they are in Indonesia and several other Muslim countries.

Text-Dependent Questions

1. How did Islam improve the status of women in the Prophet Muhammad's time?
2. What is a *hijab*?

Research Project

In recent years, as Islamist movements in many countries have stressed a return to the fundamental principals of Islam, a greater number of Muslim women have chosen to veil themselves in public. In some conservative countries, such as Afghanistan and Saudi Arabia, a woman's entire body is covered, while in secular states such as Turkey, colorful headscarves are worn but the traditional hijab garment is banned by the government. Using the internet, find out more about the practice of veiling and what it means to Muslim women. Write a two-page report about your findings, and share it with your class.

STOP FUNDING
GENOCIDE
US AID TO ISRAEL = $9.8 mil / day
BOYCOTT ISRAEL
Al - Quds Toronto
NO TO APARTHEID
RACIAL S
WRONG
WRONG I
WRO
KIL
ZION
FOR T
BEING

6

Views on Conflicts in Palestine and Syria

There are a number of conflicts taking place in the Muslim world today. The one that draws most attention in the United States is the ongoing civil war in Syria. That conflict, which began in 2011, shows no sign of stopping, despite the intervention of the United States, Russia, France, and other major world nations. But the Syrian civil war is far from the only major conflict in the Muslim world today. The fate of the Palestinian people, who live in lands occupied by the state of Israel, is another issue that is of great concern to many Muslims. Many Muslims feel that the US supports Israel at the expense of the Palestinians, and consider the United States a puppet of Israel.

Polling organizations have attempted to get a sense of what Muslims feel about these and other ongoing conflicts. One thing that their surveys have consistently shown is that US involvement in the Islamic world has often angered and offended Muslims.

Opposite: Muslims protest against the policies of the United States and the state of Israel at a 2015 rally in Toronto, Canada. US involvement in the long-running conflict between Israel and the Palestinians is a major source of tension between people of the Islamic world and the West.

The Israeli-Palestinian Dispute

The long-running dispute between Israel and the Palestinians remains a critical issue in disagreements between Muslims and the West. The state of Israel was created after the end of World War II. In 1947 the newly formed United Nations unveiled a plan to divide the region of the Middle East known as Palestine into two countries. One would be predominantly Jewish, home to Jews who had settled there during the previous century, as well as to European Jews who had survived the Nazi holocaust. The country was to be predominantly Arab, populated by people who had lived in the region for a long time. The city of Jerusalem, which has religious significance to Jews, Muslims, and Christians, was supposed to be open to all people under UN administration. The Arabs of the Middle East opposed this plan, but Jewish leaders in Palestine agreed to the *partition*. On May 15, 1948, Jewish leaders officially declared the independent state of Israel, within the boundaries delineated by the United Nations' partition plan.

Immediately, troops of five neighboring Arab countries, which had not agreed to the UN plan, attacked Israel. In fierce fighting over the next two years Israel defeated the Arab armies, winning its independence. During this 1948–49 war, tens of thousands of Palestinian Arabs fled their homes, hoping to avoid violence, terrorism, and war. By the end of the war, it is estimated that between 500,000 and 750,000 Palestinians had left their homes. Some moved during the fighting to the West Bank or Gaza Strip—territories in Palestine that were controlled by Jordan and Egypt,

Words to Understand in This Chapter

autocratic—ruled by a dictator who holds absolute power.
partition—to divide a region or a country into two or more parts.
summit—a meeting between heads of government.

respectively. Other Palestinians ended up in hastily built refugee camps in Lebanon, Syria, or Jordan.

Fighting between Israel and its neighbors continued throughout the 1950s and early 1960s. The Arab countries refused to recognize the right of Israel to exist. In June 1967, Israel feared that Egypt, Syria, and other Arab countries were preparing an attack, so it launched a pre-emptive strike against its neighbors. The surprise attack was successful, and in less than a week Israeli forces had seized a huge area of territory, including East Jerusalem and the West Bank from Jordan, the Gaza Strip and Sinai Peninsula from Egypt, and the Golan Heights from Syria.

The June 1967 War led another wave of Palestinian Arabs to leave their homes and flee to the refugee camps outside of Israel. At the same time, the Israeli occupation of East Jerusalem, the West Bank, and the Gaza Strip placed more than a million Palestinian Arabs under the control of Israel's government. Israeli troops enforced martial law throughout the occupied territories, and Palestinians were permitted few rights in Israeli society. The Israeli government also took over ownership of property left behind by Palestinian refugees, distributing the land to Jewish settlers.

Until 1967, many Palestinian Arabs—both refugees and those living in the occupied territories—had hoped that the other Arab states would help them to regain their lands by conquering Israel. After the June 1967 War it was obvious that Israel was much stronger militarily than its Arab neighbors. Although there had been Palestinian opposition groups before the war, they began to attract new followers and become more radical. Organizations like the Palestine Liberation Organization (PLO) were soon attacking Israeli targets. Israel retaliated by bombing PLO bases in Lebanon and Jordan and assassinating suspected Palestinian leaders.

The Palestinian Arab minority in Israel, which includes both Christians and Muslims, that live in Israel did not have the same freedom and opportunities as did Jewish citizens. Palestinians were not allowed to build mosques without permission from the government. They also saw a disparity in funding for education and medical services between Jewish and Arab neighborhoods. When it came to land disputes, Palestinians felt that Israeli courts favored Jewish newcomers and recent immigrants to Israel over Arab families that had established a long history in the land. Also, few Arabs were able to reach high-level governmental positions.

By the mid-1980s, Palestinian anger at the lack of progress, and at their oppressive living conditions, began to boil over. In 1987 a series of protests began in Gaza and the West Bank. This uprising became known as the *intifada*. Israeli troops responded with force to stone-throwing demonstrations by angry Palestinian civilians. According to B'Tselem, an Israeli human-rights group, more than 1,100 Palestinians and about 100 Israeli civilians were killed between 1987 and 1993.

After secret negotiations in Oslo, Norway, in 1993 Israel agreed to gradually permit limited Palestinian self-government in the occupied territories and to continue negotiations aimed at further satisfying the concerns of both parties. In September 1993, an agreement known as the Declaration of Principles was signed on the White House lawn, and sealed with a historic handshake between Israeli prime minister Yitzhak Rabin and PLO leader Yasir Arafat.

Over the next few years some progress was made toward a permanent solution to the Israeli-Palestinian problem. A provisional government, the Palestinian Authority, was formed in 1994, and the next year Israel gave the authority control over parts of the West Bank. However, extremists on both sides made a fair peace settlement difficult. In July 2000 US President Bill Clinton hosted a *summit* at Camp David between Arafat and Israeli prime minister Ehud Barak, who had been elected on a promise to create a lasting peace with the Palestinians. The talks failed.

The Palestinians were tired of waiting. In September of that year a second Palestinian *intifada* began in the occupied territories. Suicide bombing attacks by Palestinians became more common. Israel responded by replacing Palestinian self-rule with martial law, restricting Palestinian freedoms, and retaliating against

An Israeli policeman storing the remains of rockets fired into Israel from Gaza Strip. Palestinian militants have fired more than 10,000 rockets into southern Israel since 2001, resulting in many civilian casualties.

suicide attacks with military force. The prospect for peace vanished beneath new waves of terror and repression.

Palestinians pointed to the continued growth of Jewish settlements in the occupied territories as a sign that Israel had not acted in good faith during the peace process. In 1990, there had been approximately 76,000 Israeli settlers in some 150 settlements. By 2000, the population of Israeli settlements had increased to more than 200,000.

In August 2005, Israel unilaterally withdrew from its settlements in the Gaza Strip, and also dismantled four settlements in the West Bank. However, Israel also moved toward annexing about one-third of the remaining West Bank territory.

In the following years, the militant Palestinian party Hamas gained control over the Gaza Strip, which it used to launch rocket and mortar attacks against Israel. The country responded with airstrikes and military incursions of its own. In 2006 Israel attacked Lebanon, after a militia affiliated with the Lebanese Islamist party Hezbollah ambushed Israeli soldiers near the border. The Second Lebanon War claimed the lives of more than 1,000 Lebanese, most of them civilians. Israel officially reported 121 of its soldiers killed in action, with more than 40 Israeli civilians also losing their lives. Over the next decade, the pattern of rocket attacks from Gaza and Lebanon, followed by Israeli military responses, would continue.

Following elections in February 2009, Likud's Benjamin Netanyahu gained power as Israel's prime minister. Netanyahu would take a hard line on security issues, bringing the Israeli-Palestinian peace process to a virtual standstill. Tensions between the two sides occasionally boiled over into full-fledged conflict, such as in July 2014, when Israel began a massive bombing campaign targeting the Gaza Strip. A week later, Israeli ground forces entered Gaza. By the time the war ended on August 26, 66 Israeli soldiers, along with six Israeli civilians, had been killed. Meanwhile, according to the UN Office for the Coordination of Humanitarian Affairs, some 2,220 Palestinians had lost their lives—and nearly 1,500 of them were civilians. Israel was widely condemned for its failure to take steps to protect noncombatants.

As the peace process has stagnated, many Muslims have charged that the United States blindly supports Israel and what they view as its oppression of the Palestinian people. Public opinion polls have reflected this attitude. A July 2014 Pew Research Center poll found that anti-American attitudes were particularly strong in the Middle East, even in countries that have traditionally been close US allies. In Egypt, for example, only 10 percent of the people held a "favorable" view of the United States, while 85 percent held an "unfavorable" view. Support for the US was not much higher in Jordan (12 percent favorable; 85 percent unfavorable) and Turkey (19 percent favorable; 73 percent unfavorable). Only 14 percent of Pakistanis held a favorable view of the United States.

Two-State Solution

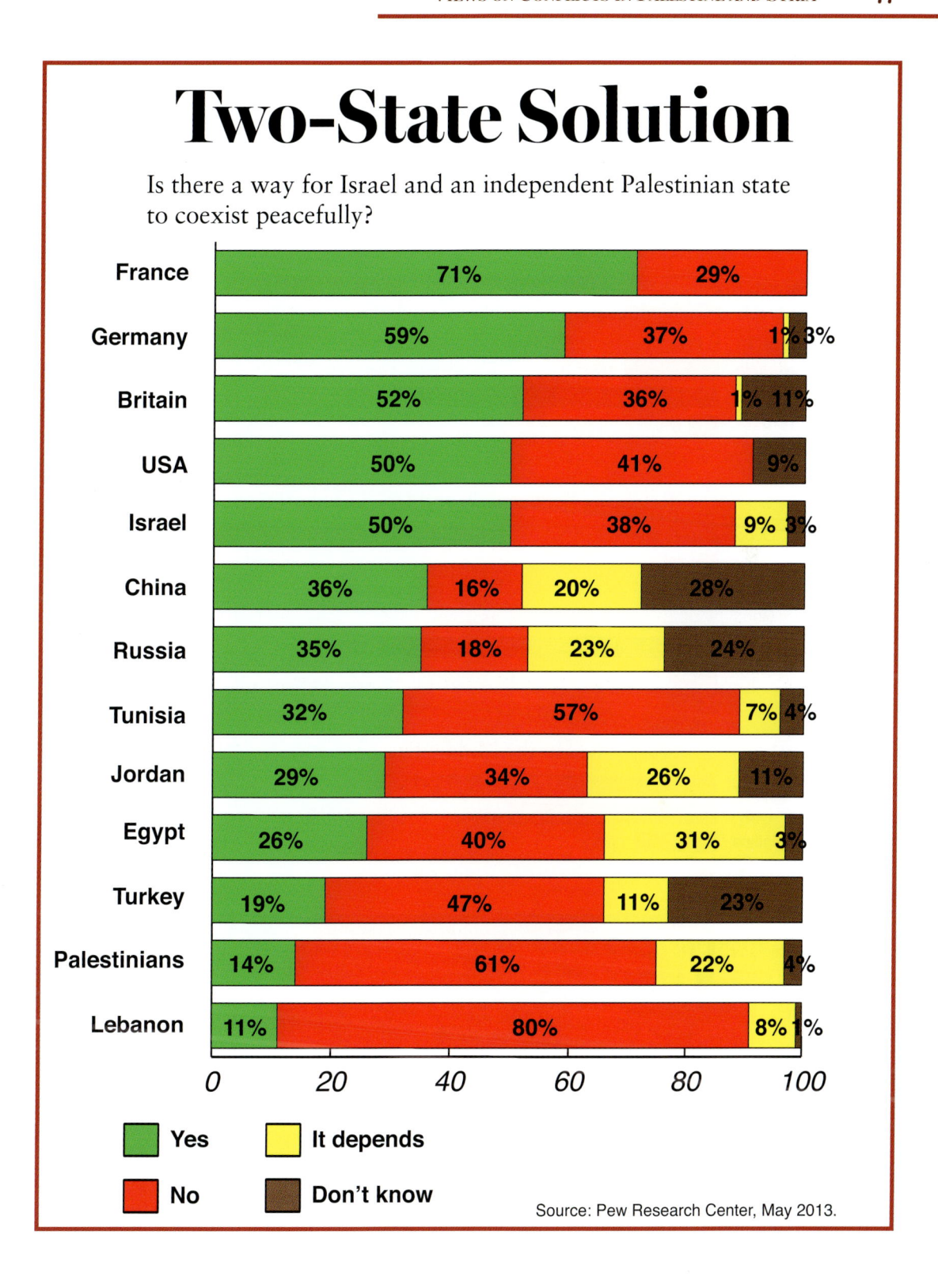

Is there a way for Israel and an independent Palestinian state to coexist peacefully?

Country	Yes	No	It depends	Don't know
France	71%	29%		
Germany	59%	37%	1%	3%
Britain	52%	36%	1%	11%
USA	50%	41%		9%
Israel	50%	38%	9%	3%
China	36%	16%	20%	28%
Russia	35%	18%	23%	24%
Tunisia	32%	57%	7%	4%
Jordan	29%	34%	26%	11%
Egypt	26%	40%	31%	3%
Turkey	19%	47%	11%	23%
Palestinians	14%	61%	22%	4%
Lebanon	11%	80%	8%	1%

Source: Pew Research Center, May 2013.

US in the Mideast

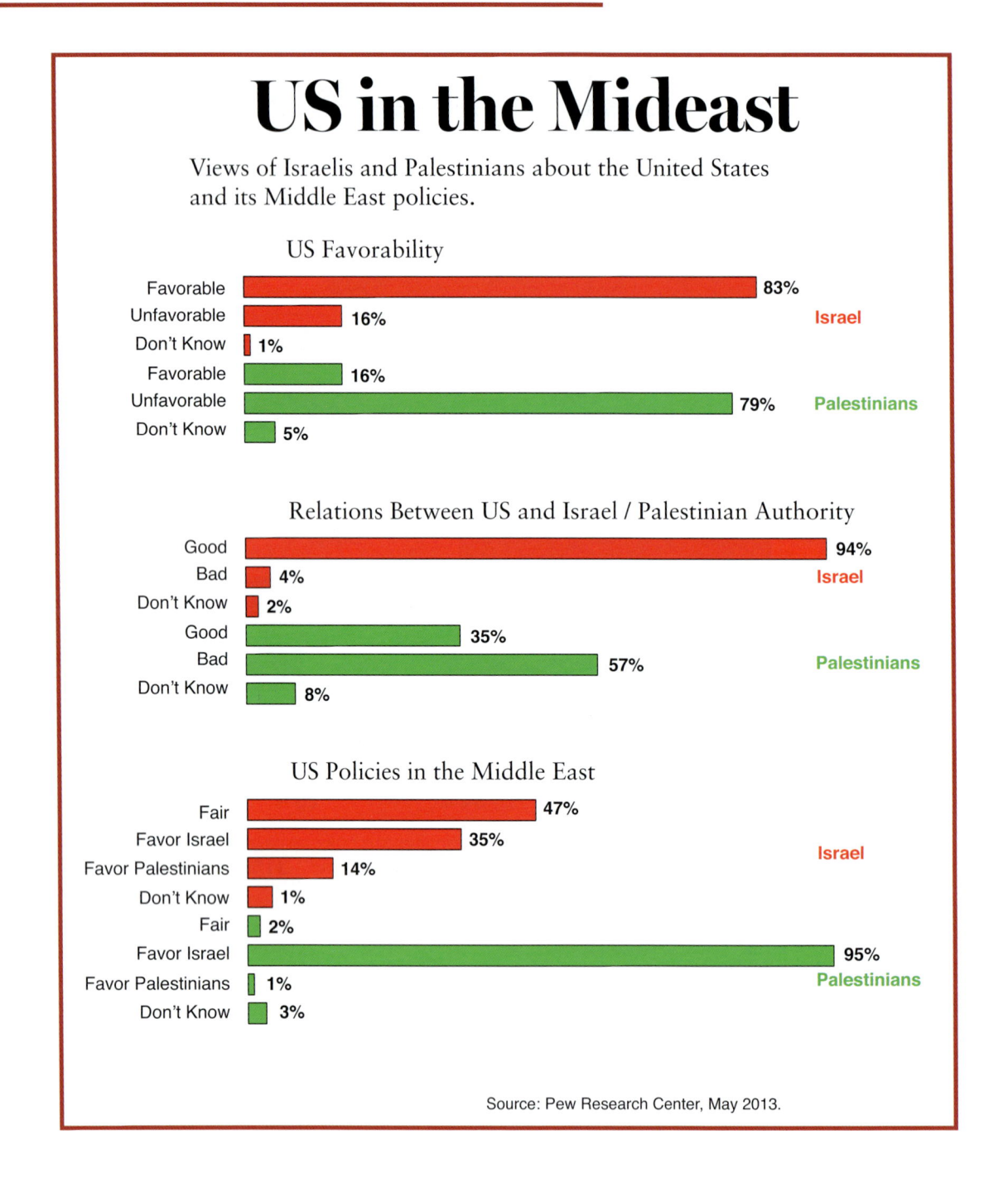

Views of Israelis and Palestinians about the United States and its Middle East policies.

US Favorability

Israel
- Favorable: 83%
- Unfavorable: 16%
- Don't Know: 1%

Palestinians
- Favorable: 16%
- Unfavorable: 79%
- Don't Know: 5%

Relations Between US and Israel / Palestinian Authority

Israel
- Good: 94%
- Bad: 4%
- Don't Know: 2%

Palestinians
- Good: 35%
- Bad: 57%
- Don't Know: 8%

US Policies in the Middle East

Israel
- Fair: 47%
- Favor Israel: 35%
- Favor Palestinians: 14%
- Don't Know: 1%

Palestinians
- Fair: 2%
- Favor Israel: 95%
- Favor Palestinians: 1%
- Don't Know: 3%

Source: Pew Research Center, May 2013.

Somewhat surprisingly, a relatively high 30 percent of Palestinians surveyed in the 2014 study viewed the US favorably, with 66 percent having unfavorable views. That was an improve-

Palestinian Views

What is the best way to achieve statehood?

- Armed Struggle: 45%
- Negotiations: 15%
- Nonviolent resistance: 15%
- Combination of all three: 15%
- Don't know: 3%

Note: Asked in the Palestinian territories only.
Source: Pew Research Center, May 2013.

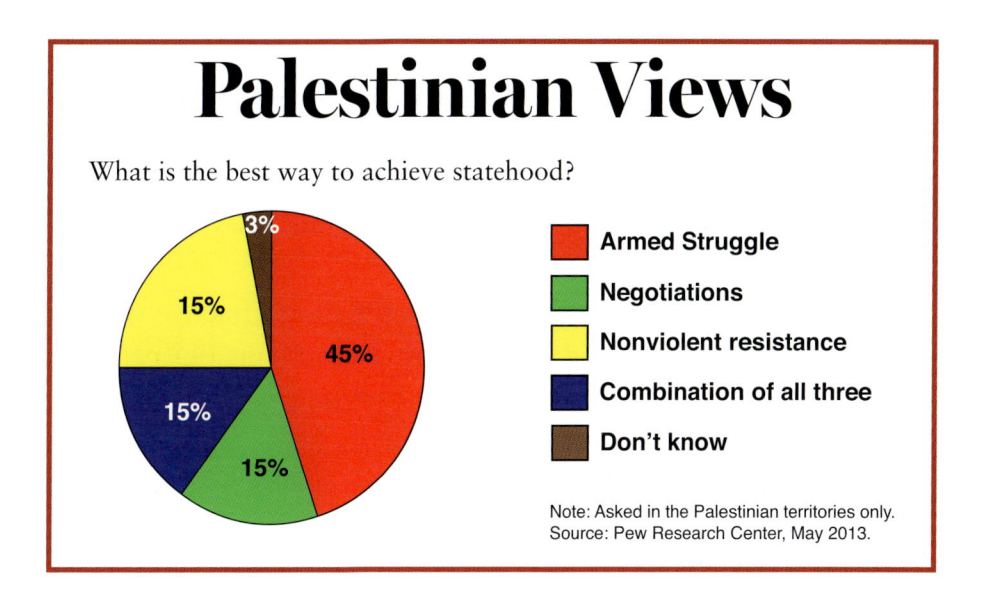

ment over a May 2013 study, in which just 14 percent of Palestinians viewed the US favorably, while 79 percent held unfavorable views of the US. In that survey, only 2 percent of Palestinians felt that the US involvement in the peace process was fair, while 95 percent believed US policies were biased toward Israel. (In Israel, meanwhile, 83 percent viewed the US favorably, and 47 percent felt its policies related to the Israel-Palestinian peace process were fair.

Israelis and Palestinians have very different opinions on the prospects for the establishment of an independent Palestinian state that can coexist peacefully alongside Israel. Half of Israelis think this is possible, while 38 percent say it is not possible and 9% chose the qualified answer "it depends." Palestinians are far less optimistic: 61 percent do not believe a way can be found for Israel and an independent Palestinian state to coexist peacefully. Fourteen percent of Palestinians say coexistence is possible, while 22 percent say it depends.

Muslims in other Middle Eastern nations are also skeptical. In neighboring Lebanon, 80 percent of those polled said there was not a way for a peaceful two-state solution to be achieved. This view was shared by 57 percent of Tunisians, 47 percent of Turks, and 40 percent of Egyptians. Of the Arab states that were polled, Jordan had the lowest rate of those who believed there was no way for Israel and an independent Palestinian state to coexist peacefully, at 34 percent, although this was still higher than the percentage of Jordanians that believed peaceful coexistence was possible (29 percent).

When asked what they thought was the most effective way to achieve true Palestinian statehood, most Palestinians (45 percent) chose the option of an armed struggle. Two other options, negotiations or nonviolent resistance, where each chosen by 15 percent of Palestinians. Another 22 percent felt that a combination of all three approaches would be most effective.

When asked about the involvement of other Arab countries in the Israel-Palestinian issue, 75 percent of Palestinians said that they were not doing enough to help the Palestinians achieve statehood. Sixteen percent said other Arab nations are doing enough, and 5 percent believed they were doing too much.

Civil War in Syria

In late 2010 and early 2011, anti-government protests began to occur in a number of Arab countries, beginning with the North African country of Tunisia. The protests—which became known as the "Arab Spring"—were aimed at improving the political circumstances and living conditions of the Arab people. They soon spread to Egypt, Bahrain, Libya, Saudi Arabia, Jordan, Yemen, and many other countries in the Middle East.

In Syria, he first sign of the Arab Spring was the appearance of graffiti in the city of Daraa that criticized the regime of Bashar al-Assad in early 2011. The Syrian government responded by arresting the students who were responsible. This led to larger protests. Inspired by successful revolutions that had overthrown the *autocratic* governments in Tunisia and Egypt, Syrian protesters used marches, hunger strikes, rioting, vandalism, and guerrilla attacks to destabilize the Assad regime. The Syrian police and military used force in an effort to quell the demonstrations, but despite the deaths of several people the unrest soon spread throughout the country.

By August 2011, the protests had turned into a violent uprising, with the United Nations and many countries condemning the Syrian government's use of heavy weaponry against rebel forces, as well as the killing of civilians. Several countries, including the United States and Turkey, began to arm and train rebel groups, while militant Islamist groups in places like Iraq and Libya began to send fighters to Syria.

In June 2012, the Free Syrian Army gained control over most of Aleppo, as well as several other cities and towns in Syria. That rebel group was formed of former Syrian Army officers and soldiers, and trained and supplied by Turkey and the US In November, representatives of the Free Syrian Army met with leaders of other rebel groups in Qatar, where they agreed to form the

A Syrian Army infantry fighting vehicle near the entrance to the town of Ma'loula. More than 220,000 people have been killed in the Syrian civil war that began in 2011.

National Coalition for Syrian Revolutionary and Opposition Forces. For the most part, Islamist groups fighting in Syria refused to join the Coalition, however.

The United States, Turkey, Great Britain, France, and more than 120 other countries soon granted official recognition to the National Coalition as the legitimate representative of the Syrian people. This added another element of international pressure to the regime, which was already dealing with economic sanctions imposed by the Arab League, the European Union, Turkey, and the United States. Beginning in 2012, the United Nations and Arab League sent several special envoys to meet with government leaders in the region and try to resolve the Syrian crisis.

The year 2013 saw the rise of a new group—the Islamic State of Iraq and the Levant (ISIL), which was able to capture and hold territory in both Iraq and Syria. That same year, the Assad government was accused of introducing chemical weapons into the civil war. This led to renewed demands for Bashar al-Assad to relinquish power, as well as a threat by US President Barack Obama to consider military options within Syria to remove the Assad regime. Under international pressure, the Syrian government agreed to destroy its chemical weapons through a U.N.-supervised process.

During 2014, the United Nations began holding peace negotiations between the Assad regime and rebel groups. However, the talks went nowhere as Bashar al-Assad refused to step down and turn over power to a transitional government. The Syrian military instead used the cease-fire to prepare for new offensives against rebel positions in Aleppo and elsewhere.

By June 2014, after conquering the city of Mosul in Iraq, ISIL declared itself to be the restoration of the Islamic caliphate. ISIL's extremist leaders claimed that all Muslims needed to swear allegiance to their organization and follow its dictates, and that Islam needed to be returned to a "pure" state by eliminating apostates, or those who do not follow their teachings. ISIL attempted to do this in the territories it controlled by murdering Christians, Jews,

Kurds, Shiite Muslims, Druze, and others living in the regions it controlled.

The reports of ISIL atrocities led the United States, Russia, Turkey, France and other countries to intervene in the Syrian civil war with military force. Airstrikes were launched against ISIL positions, although the US and other countries decided not to send in soldiers to wage ground combat.

By 2016, according to the United Nations, more than 220,000 people had been killed in the Syrian civil war, while more than 9 million Syrians—roughly half of the population—were refugees. Syrian civilians have suffered greatly during the war. A UN study found that both sides had engaged in acts that would be considered war crimes—rape, murder, and torture. The Assad regime has used "barrel bombs"—improvised explosive devices dropped from aircraft—to devastate both civilian and rebel populations and turn Syria's once-proud cities into rubble. Tragically, it appears this conflict will not end any time soon.

One of ISIL's stated goals is to bring about a clash with the non-Muslim world, which according to its beliefs the Muslims are destined to win. ISIL's atrocities against Christians and westerners has been devoted to this end, along with its destruction of ancient historical sites in Syria and other lands it rules. The group has destroyed Shiite mosques and shrines in Iraq, as well as Christian churches and monasteries. The group has also destroyed ancient ruins, including a pagan temple and a Roman theater in Palmyra, Syria, and structures built during the Assyrian period that date back more than 2,500 years.

ISIL has also attempted to attack the West directly, in hopes of inciting an invasion by ground troops in response. In 2015 and 2016, members of the group carried out terrorist attacks in many countries outside of Iraq and Syria, including a mass shooting at a Tunisian resort, several bombings in Turkey and Lebanon, and the destruction of a Russian airliner carrying 224 people. The November 2015 Paris attacks killed 130 people, while March 2016 bombings in Brussels, Belgium, and at a soccer stadium in

Iraq each killed more than 30 civilians.

A Pew Research Center poll conducted in November 2015, after several of these terrorist attacks, showed that many Muslims held overwhelmingly negative views of ISIL. The data was collected in 10 countries with significant Muslim populations, including Burkina Faso, Indonesia, Jordan, Lebanon, Malaysia, Nigeria, Pakistan, the Palestinian territories, Senegal, and Turkey. In Lebanon, nearly every person polled had an unfavorable view of the Islamic State, possibly because the Pew survey was taken shortly after an ISIL suicide bombing in a Shiite Muslim neighborhood near Beirut killed forty-three people and injured more than 200. In no country surveyed did more than 15 percent of the population show favorable attitudes toward Islamic State. However, in Pakistan more than 60 percent of the people who responded to the poll said they did not know enough about the group to answer.

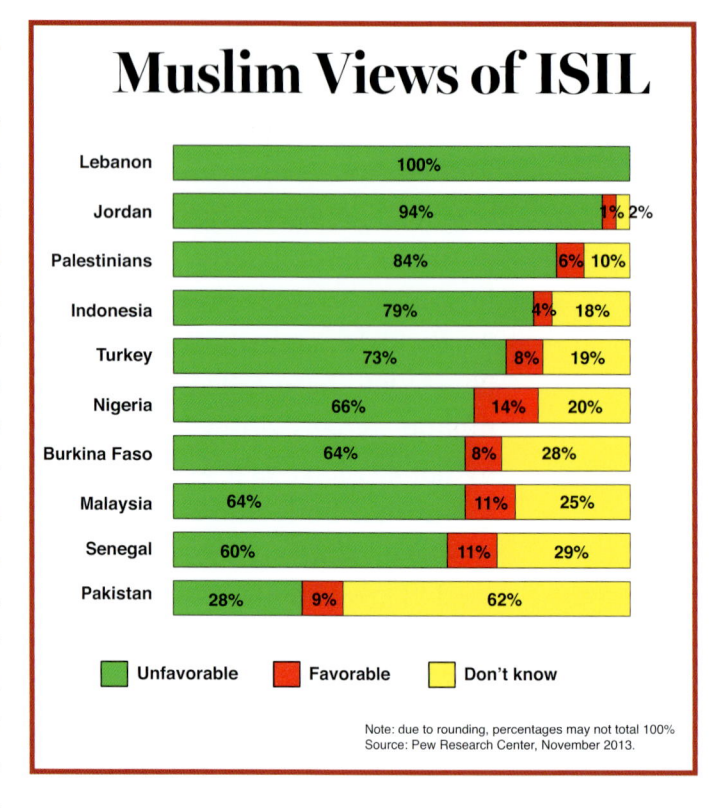

Muslim Views of ISIL

Country	Unfavorable	Favorable	Don't know
Lebanon	100%		
Jordan	94%	1%	2%
Palestinians	84%	6%	10%
Indonesia	79%	4%	18%
Turkey	73%	8%	19%
Nigeria	66%	14%	20%
Burkina Faso	64%	8%	28%
Malaysia	64%	11%	25%
Senegal	60%	11%	29%
Pakistan	28%	9%	62%

Note: due to rounding, percentages may not total 100%
Source: Pew Research Center, November 2013.

Compared to the other countries, Nigerians had the highest level of support for ISIL (14 percent favorable). However, opinions of the group differed sharply by religious affiliation. Seventy-one percent of Nigerian Christians had an unfavorable view of ISIS, as did 61 percent of Nigerian Muslims. However, 20 percent of Nigerian Muslims had a favorable view of ISIS, while only 7 percent of Christians viewed the group favorably. An Islamist group in Nigeria that calls itself Boko Haram has been regularly attacking Christian villages in the country since 2009. Boko

Haram has pledged allegiance to the Islamic State.

Internationally, a Pew Research Center poll from June 2015 showed that people in most countries of the world supported the US military campaign against ISIL. Despite American unpopularity in many Middle East countries, the airstrikes against ISIL were supported by more than 75 percent of people in Jordan and Lebanon, both of which share a border with Syria. Muslims in other nations—including 70 percent of Nigerians and 64 percent of Indonesians—also supported US involvement. Malaysia and Pakistan were notable opponents. In Malaysia, 48 percent felt the US should not get involved, while just 28 percent supported the airstrikes. In Pakistan 33 percent opposed the US campaign against ISIL, while 16 percent supported it.

A 2014 Pew study found that most people in Egypt, Lebanon, Jordan, the Palestinian territories, Tunisia, and Turkey have a "very unfavorable" view of Syrian ruler Bashar al-Assad. Most of those surveyed said they would like him to step down—an action the dictator has shown no sign of taking. But even if Assad should relinquish power, the struggle between Syria's various factions, including the Islamic State, does not appear likely to end any time soon.

Text-Dependent Questions

1. What percentage of Palestinians feel that US policies are biased toward Israel? What percentage believe US policies are fair?
2. Who is the president of Syria?

Research Project

During the Syrian civil war, a major battle was fought for control over Palmyra, an ancient city. Find newspaper and magazine reports about the battle. What were the objectives of the factions that were fighting for control of the city? Did they achieve their goals? How was the civilian population of Palmyra affected? How was the local infrastructure affected? Write a two-page report and share it with your class.

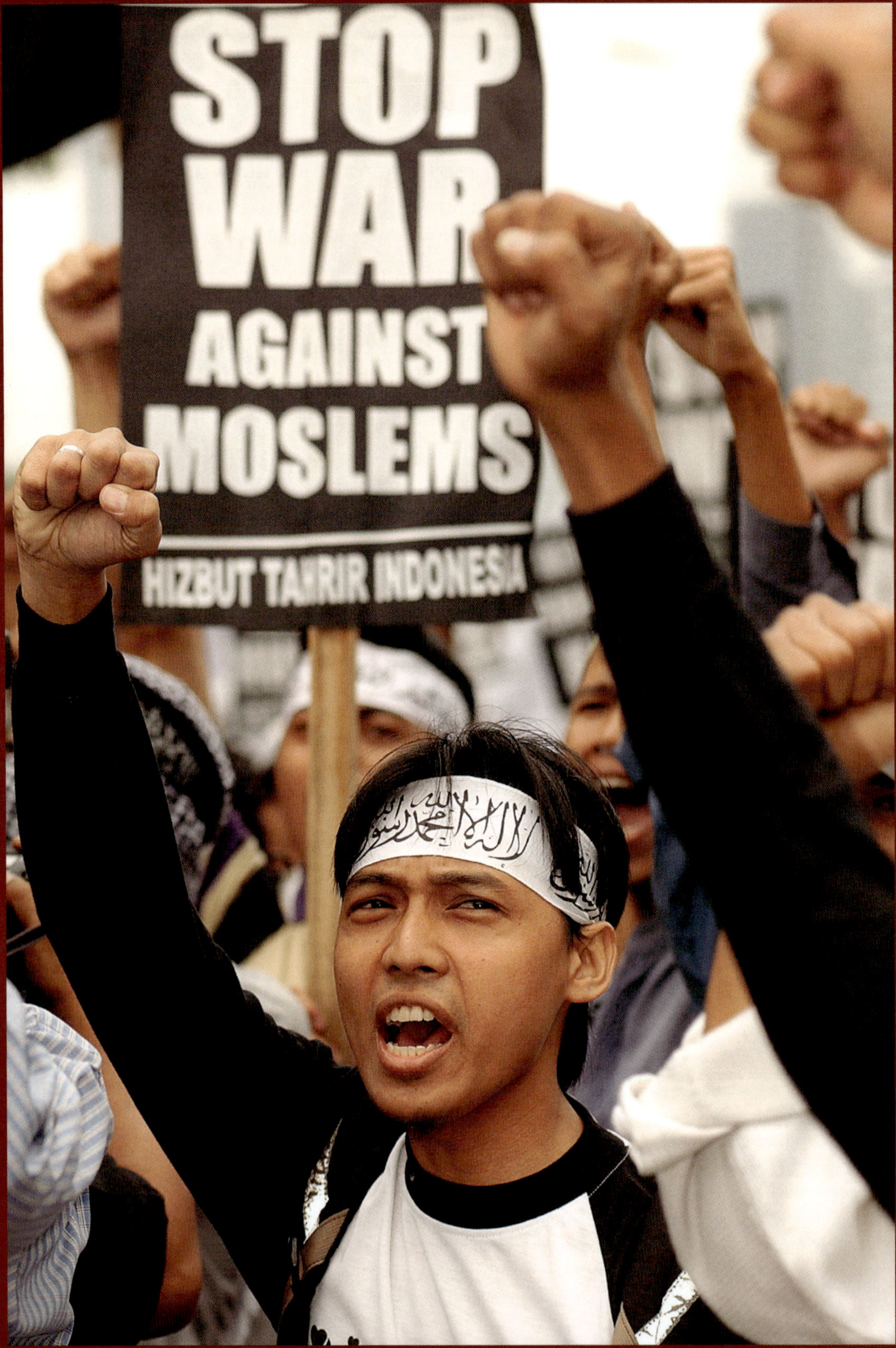
STOP WAR AGAINST MOSLEMS
HIZBUT TAHRIR INDONESIA

7
Muslim Views on Other Issues

I n general, people who live in the United States feel that their country defends freedom and democracy, and that the US gives generously to less-fortunate nations. Most US citizens are likely to view their society as trustworthy, friendly, and compassionate toward poorer nations. By contrast, as noted previously, most Muslims who respond to opinion polls have strongly unfavorable views of the United States and other Western nations.

"It is evident from the data reviewed in this project that the people of Islamic countries around the world have significant **grievances** with the West in general and with the United States in particular," commented Gallup editor-in-chief Frank Newport at the time of the original Gallup Survey of the Muslim world in 2001-02. "At almost every opportunity within the survey, respondents overwhelmingly agree that the United States is aptly described by such negative labels as ruthless, aggressive, conceited, arrogant, easily provoked, biased. . . . The people of Islamic nations also believe that Western nations do

Opposite: Indonesian Muslims demonstrate outside the US embassy in Jakarta to protest against the looming war against Iraq, January 2003. Many people in the Islamic world have unfavorable views of the United States, particularly in its attitude toward Muslim nations.

not respect Arab or Islamic values, do not support Arabs causes, and do not exhibit fairness toward . . . Muslims."

The Pew Research Center's studies have tended to reinforce this view. In a 2011 Pew survey of seven countries with Muslims majorities, Muslims said they viewed Westerners as "selfish" (68 percent of those polled), "greedy (66 percent), or "immoral (61 percent). Relatively few Muslims attributed positive characteristics, such as "respectful of women" (44 percent), "honest" (33 percent), and "tolerant" (31 percent) to Westerners.

The United States became deeply involved in world affairs after World War II, during a time of rising global tensions with the Union of Soviet Socialist Republics (USSR). During this period, a major concern of US foreign policy was to prevent the Soviet Union from expanding its influence. To achieve this, the US and other western powers at times supported oppressive governments in Muslim countries and elsewhere because these governments opposed the Soviet Union and *communism*. In much of the Islamic world, Muslims still resent the US for its foreign-policy actions during the past fifty years.

Views on Western Values

The imposition of Western culture and values on the civilization of the Islamic world is a sore spot for many Muslims. People have argued that the influence of western values and exposure to west-

Words to Understand in This Chapter

communism—a political theory derived from the writings of Karl Marx which advocated a revolution by the working classes that would lead to a society in which all property is publicly owned and each person works and is paid according to their abilities and needs.

grievance—a real or imagined wrong or other cause for complaint or protest, especially unfair treatment.

A Sri Lankan Muslim man in traditional dress.

ern media, with its graphic depictions of violence, drug and alcohol abuse, and extramarital sex, undermines the culture of the Islamic world. Many people in the Islamic world agree over this matter, viewing the West as materialistic and indifferent to religious values. At the same time, however, they acknowledge the positive aspects of Western culture, such as advances in science and technology, and see western nations as educationally and economically advanced.

One question in the Gallup Organization's survey of the Islamic world asked, "How positively or negatively do you think our own value system is being influenced by the value system that prevails in the Western societies." Respondents were given a five-point scale, ranging from "very positive" to "neither" to "very negative." Most of those who answered felt that the western influence was negative.

The Influence of Western Values

	Positive: Very	Positive: Somewhat	Negative: Somewhat	Negative: Very	Neither
Kuwait	7%	19%	26%	22%	22%
Saudi Arabia	8%	12%	22%	31%	16%
Indonesia	9%	11%	32%	16%	29%
Lebanon	5%	11%	22%	40%	21%
Iran	5%	11%	19%	20%	23%
Turkey	2%	8%	24%	21%	16%
Morocco	1%	9%	49%	18%	10%
Pakistan	4%	5%	17%	27%	12%
Jordan	3%	3%	21%	53%	20%

Source: The Gallup Organization.

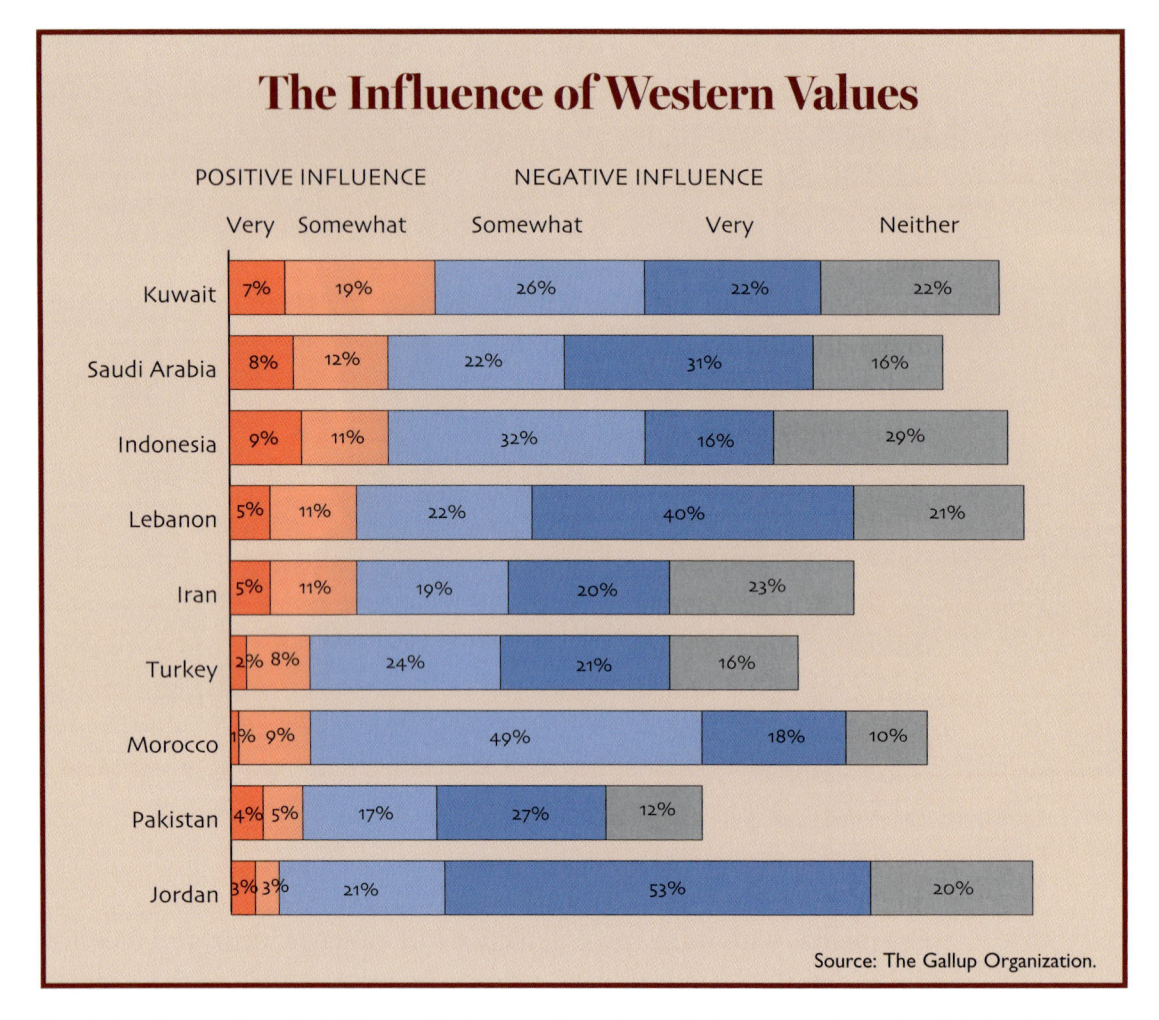

The Gallup Organization asked, "How positively or negatively do you think our own value system is being influenced by the value system that prevails in the Western societies?" As this chart reflects, in every country the views of Muslims toward the United States were more negative than positive.

In Jordan, a country that is considered moderate and friendly by the United States, 74 percent of those who responded said that western influence was negative—53 percent "very negative," 21 percent "somewhat negative." Just 6 percent felt the Western influence was positive, while 20 percent answered "neither." In Morocco, 67 percent felt that western influence is negative (18 percent "very," 49 percent "somewhat"), while this was the case among 62 percent of Lebanese respondents (40 percent "very," 22 percent "somewhat"). In Morocco, less than 1 percent of the respondents felt that western values have a "very positive" influence—the lowest figure in the survey.

The lowest percentage of people with a negative opinion of western values was in Iran, a country where more than 20 years ago the people overthrew the western-supported government of the shah and replaced it with an Islamic theocracy. In Iran, 39 percent of respondents felt a negative influence of western values (20 percent "very," 19 percent "somewhat").

The country with the highest percent of respondents that favored western values was Kuwait, at 26 percent (7 percent "very positive," 19 percent "somewhat positive"). This was still significantly lower than the 48 percent of Kuwaitis that felt western values have a negative influence. Indonesia was next, with 20 percent feeling that western values have a positive effect (9 percent "very," 12 percent "somewhat"), with Saudi Arabia also at 20 percent (8 percent "very," 12 percent "somewhat"), and Lebanon and Iran at 16 percent (in both countries, 5 percent felt the impact was "very positive," while 11 percent found it "somewhat positive").

In Turkey, perhaps the one country studied in the Gallup survey that is most similar socially to a European state, just 10 percent of the population felt that western values have a positive influence (2 percent "very," 8 percent "somewhat"). By contrast, 45 percent of Turks felt that western values have a negative influence (21 percent "very," 24 percent "somewhat").

Views on Terrorism

People in the West often link terrorism to Muslims. Western perceptions of Islam have been shaped by media coverage of suicide bombings in Israel and the occupied territories, by the violence of the 1979 Iranian Revolution, and by attacks on US targets like the 1993 World Trade Center bombing, the 1998 attack on US embassies in Kenya and Tanzania, the 2000 blast that damaged the US warship *Cole* in the harbor at Aden, Yemen, and of course the

September 11, 2001, attacks on the World Trade Center and the Pentagon. More recent attacks by Muslim terrorists include the November 2015 attacks in Paris, killed 137 people and wounded 368. This attack—like subsequent attacks in Istanbul, Brussels, Beirut, and other cities—was carried out by Muslim extremists inspired by the Islamic State of Iraq and the Levant (ISIL). Other notable terrorist attacks conducted by extremists in the name of Islam include the Boston Marathon bombing in 2013; the attack on the U.S. embassy in Benghazi, Libya, in 2012; and the Fort Hood shooting in 2009, in which a Muslim military officer killed 13 American soldiers. These are just a few of the dozens of terrorist attacks that are committee each year by Muslim extremists.

The truth is, however, that most Muslims do not support terrorism, and the perception that many Muslims are terrorists is unfair and incorrect. Terrorism and other forms of violence hap-

A Muslim vendor sells tomatoes on a street of Old Delhi, India.

Turkish Muslims fish from the Galata Bridge in Istanbul.

pen throughout the world, not just among Muslims. Historically, many groups and organizations throughout the world have used terrorism as a political tool. Even today there are many non-Muslim terrorist groups—various Roman Catholic and Protestant groups in Northern Ireland; Basque separatists in Spain; rebel guerrillas like FARC and ELN in Colombia; and leftist organizations like Tupac Amaru in Peru.

There have been terrorist attacks carried out by non-Muslim Americans in the United States, such as the 1995 bombing of a federal office building in Oklahoma City. An FBI study found that non-Muslims committed 94 percent of the terrorist acts that occurred in the United States between 1980 and 2005. And a 2014 study conducted by the University of North Carolina found that since September 11, Muslim-linked terrorism had claimed the lives of 37 Americans. In that same time period, more than

A Muslim woman in Mandalay, Myanmar, carries her goods home from the local market. The Muslim Rohingya people of Myanmar have been persecuted by the Buddhist majority of that country for many years.

190,000 Americans were murdered.

Most Muslims agree that their religion forbids the killing of innocent civilians. They cite scripture passages like Qur'an 2: 190, which commands believers to "fight for the sake of God those that fight against you, but do not attack them first. God does not love the aggressors."

"Peace is the essence of Islam," says Prince El Hassan bin Talal of Jordan, a descendent of Muhammad. "Respecting the sanctity of life is the cornerstone of our faith." Saudi Arabia's highest authority on Islamic law, Shaikh Abdulaziz Al-Ashaikh, agrees. Shortly after the September 11 attacks, he said, "The recent developments in the United States, including hijacking planes, terrorizing innocent people, and shedding blood, constitute a form of injustice that cannot be tolerated by Islam, which views them as gross crimes and sinful acts."

Nevertheless, the issue of terrorism is a major problem confronting the Islamic world today. The debate over the causes of terrorism heated up considerably after the September 11 attacks. Some believe Muslim terrorists act out of frustration with the lack of freedom and economic opportunities in their countries. Others see terrorism as inspired by religious fervor or anger at Western colonialism and oppression.

Muslim terrorists sometimes justify their actions by claiming that they are supported by Islam. Islamic terrorists introduced Americans to the Arabic word *jihad*, which is usually translated as "holy war." But *jihad* actually means any effort to support Islam or do what is right for a Muslim, not necessarily a war.

With the rise of groups like the Islamic State in Syria and Iraq, Muslims around the world are becoming more concerned about extremism conducted in the name of their religion, including terrorist attacks. A July 2015 survey by the Pew Research Center found that a growing number of people in ten majority-Muslim countries reported that they were "very concerned" about extremism and terrorism in their country.

In this survey, Nigeria had the highest percentage of people who were "very concerned," at 68 percent. This may well be due to the activities of the Islamist group known as Boko Haram. Roughly translated, the group's name means "Western influence is a sin," and its goal is to turn Nigeria into a state governed by their vision of Islamic law. Beginning in 2009, Boko Haram initiated a terror campaign in northeastern Nigeria that resulted in hundreds of deaths. Although government forces killed the group's leader in mid-2009, the group soon re-emerged. Since 2010, it has been waging an insurgency that has resulted in 20,000 deaths and 2.3 million Nigerians displaced from their homes. The group has carried out mass abductions, including the kidnapping of 276 schoolgirls from Chibok in April 2014. In March 2015, leaders of Boko Haram declared their allegiance to the Islamic State of Iraq and the Levant (ISIL). Consequently, between 2013 (when ISIL began to attract attention) and 2015, concerns about extremism in Nigeria

Concern about Extremism

Percentage saying they are "very concerned" about Islamic extremism in their country.

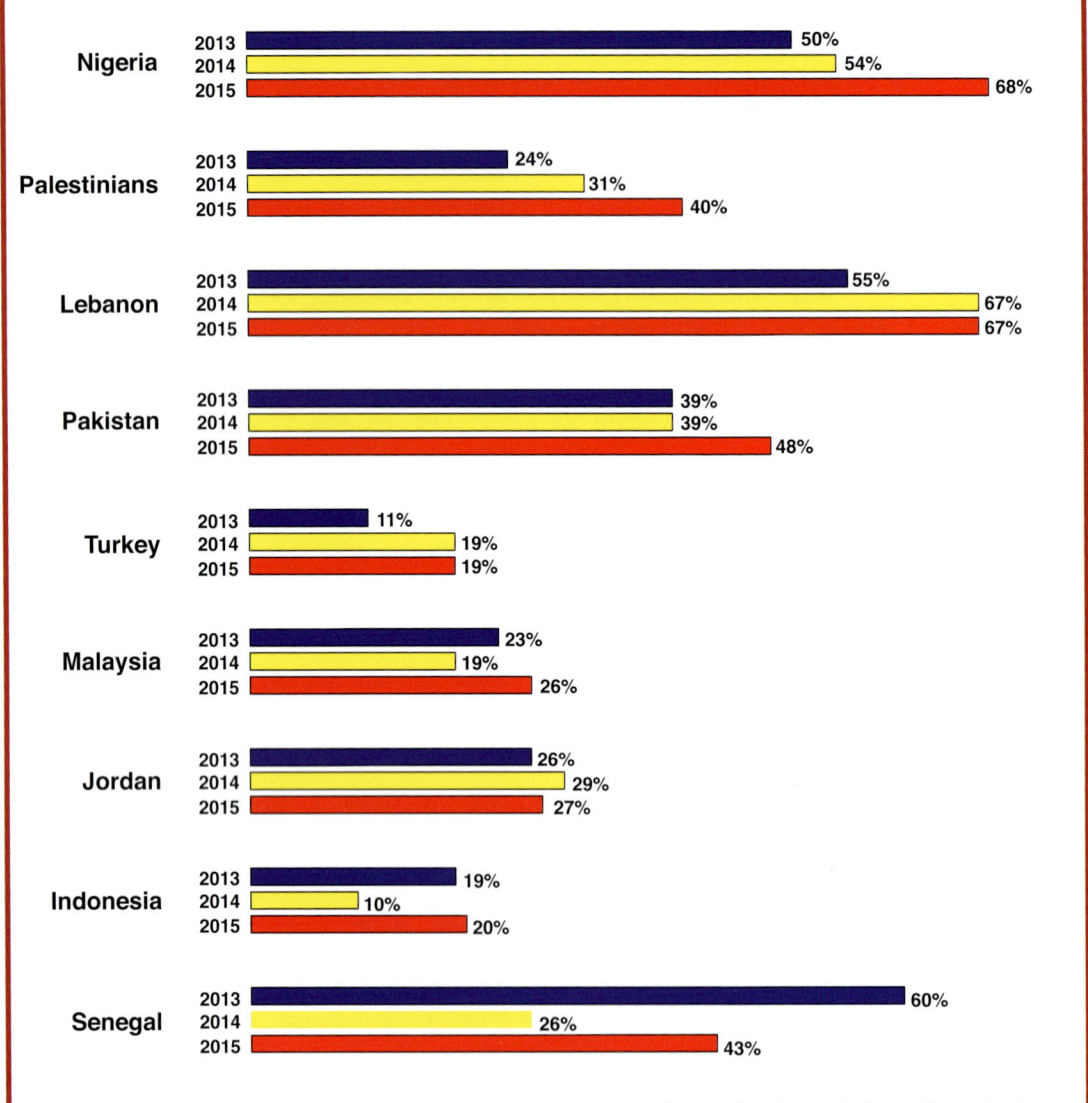

Nigeria
- 2013: 50%
- 2014: 54%
- 2015: 68%

Palestinians
- 2013: 24%
- 2014: 31%
- 2015: 40%

Lebanon
- 2013: 55%
- 2014: 67%
- 2015: 67%

Pakistan
- 2013: 39%
- 2014: 39%
- 2015: 48%

Turkey
- 2013: 11%
- 2014: 19%
- 2015: 19%

Malaysia
- 2013: 23%
- 2014: 19%
- 2015: 26%

Jordan
- 2013: 26%
- 2014: 29%
- 2015: 27%

Indonesia
- 2013: 19%
- 2014: 10%
- 2015: 20%

Senegal
- 2013: 60%
- 2014: 26%
- 2015: 43%

Source: Pew Research Center, November 2015.

have risen by 18 percentage points. When Pew broke down the data, it found that 73 percent of Nigerian Christians were "very concerned" about extremists, compared to 63 percent of Nigerian Muslims.

In Lebanon, which like Nigeria is home to multiple religious groups, concerns about extremism have risen 12 percentage points since 2013. By 2015, 67 percent of Lebanese surveyed said they were "very concerned" about extremism. This concern is reflected in all segments of society—Christians (70 percent), Shiite Muslims (66 percent), and Sunni Muslims (60 percent).

In Africa, a majority of those in Burkina Faso (56 percent) were very worried about extremism, and this fear was shared by Christians and Muslims alike. In Senegal, the share of people who are very concerned fluctuated from 60 percent in 2013, when there was an imminent threat from extremists in neighboring Mali, to 26 percent in 2014, before the Islamic State established itself in the region, and back up to 43 percent in 2015, when violence from extremist groups such as Boko Haram increased across the region.

In general, Pew found that there were few variations on concern about extremism by age and gender within Muslim countries.

Conclusion

Westerners who know little about Muslims need to learn more about the Islamic world. Muslims need to learn more about Americans and the West. Both groups will soon find that they have much more in common than they thought.

The first step in understanding is to eliminate the misunderstanding and hatred that keep each group from learning the truth about the other. After the September 11 attacks, many US citizens were angry and wanted revenge. Innocent Muslim Americans were targeted for violence, even though such leaders as President George W. Bush urged Americans not to attack their fellow citizens. At the same time, it is obvious that people in Muslim countries do not see world events in the same way that

Americans do.

To learn more about each other, both groups should examine their beliefs about the other and not allow anger to disrupt their thoughts. A person who wants to better understand the Islamic world and its people better should ask himself or herself several questions:

> Because the Islamic world is very large and complex, and the lives and views of Muslims differ, am I being careful not to judge all Muslims by what I learn about a few?

A Muslim-American woman speaks at a meeting in Brooklyn. The Muslim community in the United States is growing in importance; at over 3.3 million Muslims, it is the third-largest religious group in the country, making up about 1 percent of the total US population.

Am I accepting everything I hear or read as the truth without thinking, or am I considering the information with a critical eye?

Do the facts I have learned so far make a complete picture, or is something missing?

Am I learning from people or books that are dishonest, uninformed, outdated, or irrational, or am I seeking out reliable sources, such as trustworthy books and teachers, experts, and Muslims themselves?

Both the Islamic world and the West would benefit by working to understand each other better and searching for commonalities that bring cooperation, whether it is between nations or neighbors. Across the United States and around the world, students and others are beginning the search by reaching out to their neighbors and making an effort to learn more about other people and their cultures.

Text-Dependent Questions

1. What are some reasons that people in the West often link terrorism to Muslims?
2. What does *jihad* mean?

Research Project

There are many different definitions of what terrorism is. Each person in your class should research recent news items to find examples of terrorist acts. Discuss these examples. Keeping in mind the contexts of the attacks, as well as the ideologies of the groups that committed them, what are the common elements, and how is each one different? Ask members of the group to try to define terrorism, and discuss the pros and cons of each definition. Consider the following questions: What differentiates terrorists from warriors, freedom fighters, or patriots? Is any attack on civilians a terrorist act? When governments bomb cities, is it terrorism?

Chronology

610   Muhammad receives the first revelations from Allah, which will later be recorded in the Qur'an.

613   Muhammad begins publicly preaching Allah's message.

622   Muhammad and his followers begin the *hijra*, or migration, from Mecca to Medina, an event that marks the beginning of the Muslim era.

630   An Arab Muslim army led by Muhammad takes control of Mecca.

632   Muhammad dies, and the era of the "rightly guided caliphs" begins when Abu Bakr is chosen as the first caliph.

656   Ali becomes the fourth caliph, sparking a civil war in the Muslim community.

661   Ali is assassinated, and Muawiyya declares himself caliph. Ali's supporters, the Shiites, continue to support his sons' claim to the caliphate.

680   Ali's son Hussein is killed, with his family and many supporters, at the Battle of Karbala.

683   The Umayyad succession of caliphs begins. Based in Syria, their rule extends eastward to the borders of India and China and westward to Spain.

749   The Abbasids overthrow the Umayyads.

820   al-Shafii, who created an authoritative methodology for developing *Sharia*, dies.

874   The power of the Abbasid caliphs begins to wane; local dynasties start to establish rule throughout the Abbasid empire.

1058   The jurist and mystic al-Ghazali is born; he eventually helps make Sufism accepted by mainstream Islam.

Chronology

1099 The European Crusaders capture Jerusalem and establish four Crusader kingdoms.

1187 Muslim forces under Saladin defeat the Crusaders and recapture Jerusalem.

1453 The armies of the Ottoman Turks capture Constantinople, bringing the thousand-year rule of the Byzantine empire to an end.

1502 The Safavid Empire is established in Iran; Shia Islam becomes the state religion.

1526 The Moghul Empire is founded in India.

1765 Great Britain forces the Moghul emperor to give up control of part of India; the British will eventually control all of the area of modern-day India and Pakistan.

1919 In the conference that ends World War I, the Arab lands of the defeated Ottoman empire are divided into small states and placed under the control of France or Great Britain.

1923 Turkey establishes the first secular government in a Muslim country.

1928 Hasan al-Banna founds the Muslim Brotherhood in Egypt.

1941 Mawlana Abu al-Ala Mawdudi establishes the Islamic Society in India.

1947 Pakistan is created as an Islamic state.

1948 Israel is founded, and immediately fights a two-year war for independence with its neighbors.

1967 Israel defeats the combined forces of Egypt, Jordan, and Syria in the Six-Day War.

1978 US President Jimmy Carter helps to negotiate a historic peace treaty between Israel and Egypt.

Chronology

1979   Revolution grips Iran and the Islamic Republic comes to power.

1980   Iraq invades Iran, setting off an eight-year conflict in the Persian Gulf.

1991   An international coalition of nations, led by the United States, attacks Iraq, forcing it to withdraw from Kuwait, which it had invaded and annexed in 1990.

1993   After secret negotiations in Oslo, Norway, representatives of Israel and the Palestinians establish a framework for an end to violence and the eventual establishment of an autonomous Palestinian state.

1995   During ethnic fighting in Bosnia, Serbian troops overrun a U.N. "safe area" at Srebrenica; an estimated 7,000 Muslim men and boys are massacred and buried in mass graves.

2000   The Israeli-Palestinian peace process fails, and the second *intifada* begins.

2001   On September 11, terrorists crash hijacked airplanes into the World Trade Center in New York and the Pentagon near Washington, D.C.; the US responds by attacking Afghanistan and overthrowing the Taliban regime, which had sheltered the al-Qaeda terrorist network. This action is condemned by many Muslims.

2003   In March, the United States attacks Iraq to remove Saddam Hussein from power.

2005   The Fiqh Council of North America issues a *fatwa* condemning terrorism and religious extremism.

2007   In January, Keith Ellison is sworn in to the US House of Representatives, becoming the first Muslim member of Congress.

Chronology

2008 In November, members of the Islamist terrorist group Lashkar-e-Taiba attack multiple sites in Mumbai, India. More than 250 people are killed.

2012 Mohamed Morsi, a member of the Muslim Brotherhood, is sworn in as president after he wins Egypt's first competitive presidential election. Morsi would be ousted in June of the following year by a military coup.

2013 Islamist groups fighting in Iraq and Syria form the Islamic State of Iraq and the Levant (ISIL), which is able to capture and hold territory in both countries.

2014 In June, the Islamic State of Iraq and the Levant declares a caliphate in the territory they control, stretching from Aleppo in northwestern Syria to the eastern Iraqi province of Diyala. They rename their group Islamic State (IS), although most Western observers continue to refer to the group as ISIL.

2015 The United States and other Western nations strike an agreement with the Islamic Republic of Iran, in which they agree to lift economic sanctions and restrictions on oil sales in exchange for Iran eliminating its program to build nuclear weapons. Throughout the year, terrorists who claim allegiance to ISIL commit numerous attacks, including the destruction of a airliner from Egypt carring more than 200 Russian citizens; mass shootings in Paris that kill 130 people; and an attack on a holiday party in San Bernardino, California, that kills 14 people and injures 22.

2016 Tensions between Iran and Saudi Arabia rise after King Salman orders the execution of a Shiite cleric, Nimr al-Nimr, along with 46 other dissidents.

Series Glossary

BCE and CE—alternatives to the traditional Western designation of calendar eras, which used the birth of Jesus as a dividing line. BCE stands for "Before the Common Era," and is equivalent to BC ("Before Christ"). Dates labeled CE, or "Common Era," are equivalent to Anno Domini (AD, or "the Year of Our Lord").

hadith—the body of customs, sayings, and traditions ascribed to the prophet Muhammad and his closest companions in the early Muslim community, as recorded by those who witnessed them.

hajj—the fifth pillar of Islam; a pilgrimage to Mecca, which all Muslims who are able are supposed to make at least once in their lifetime.

imam—a Muslim spiritual leader. In the Sunni tradition, an imam is a religious leader who leads the community in prayer. In the Shiite tradition, an imam is a descendant of Muhammad who is the divinely chosen and infallible leader of the community.

jihad—struggle. To Muslims, the "greater jihad" refers to an individual's struggle to live a pure life, while the "lesser jihad" refers to defensive struggle or warfare against oppression and the enemies of Islam.

Qur'an—Islam's holy scriptures, which contain Allah's revelations to the prophet Muhammad in the early seventh century.

Sharia—a traditional system of Islamic law based on the Qur'an, the opinion of Islamic leaders, and the desires of the community.

Shia—one of the two major sects of Islam; members of this sect are called Shiites.

Sufism—a mystical tradition that emphasizes the inner aspect of spirituality through meditation and remembrance of God.

Sunna—the traditions of the prophet Muhammad as exemplified by his actions and words, and preserved in the Qur'an and Hadith.

Sunni—the largest sect of Islam; the name is derived from the Arabic phrase "the Path," referring to those who follow the instructions of Muhammad as recorded in the Qur'an and other ancient writings or traditions.

umma—the worldwide community of Muslims.

Further Reading

Ali-Karamali, Sumbul. *Growing Up Muslim: Understanding the Beliefs and Practices of Islam*. Chicago: Ember, 2013.

Aslan, Reza. *No god but God: The Origins, Evolution, and Future of Islam*. New York: Random House, 2011.

Esposito, John L., and Dalia Mogahed. *Who Speaks for Islam: What a Billion Muslims Really Think*. New York: Gallup Press, 2008.

Harris, Sam, and Maajid Nawaz. *Islam and the Future of Tolerance: A Dialogue*. Cambridge, Mass.: Harvard University Press, 2015.

McCants, William. *The ISIS Apocalypse: The History, Strategy, and Doomsday Vision of the Islamic State*. New York: St. Martin's Press, 2015.

Mandaville, Peter. *Islam and Politics*. New York: Routledge, 2014.

Mansfield, Peter. *A History of the Middle East*. 4th ed. revised and updated by Nicholas Pelham. New York: Penguin Books, 2013.

Osman, Tarek. *Islamism: What it Means for the Middle East and the World*. New Haven, Conn.: Yale University Press, 2016.

Internet Resources

http://www.pbs.org/wgbh/pages/frontline/shows/muslims

A special installment of the PBS program Frontline that examines contemporary Islam through profiles of and interviews with Muslims in the United States, Africa, the Middle East, and Asia.

http://www.pewresearch.org/topics/muslims-and-islam

This page run by the Pew Research Center provides links to polls and articles about the opinions and attitudes of people living in the Muslim World.

https://www.cia.gov/library/publications/the-world-factbook

The CIA World Factbook is a convenient source of basic information about any country in the world. This site includes links to a page on each country with geographic, demographic, economic, and governmental data.

http://america.aljazeera.com

The English-language website of the Arabic news service Al Jazeera provides articles and videos on breaking news, as well as feature stories that provide background material, including profiles of leaders and essays reacting to major events.

http://islam.com

A portal with information about Islam, including discussion forums, articles, and links to other resources.

http://islam.uga.edu

A comprehensive collection of essays and links to online sources on Islamic history, culture, sects, law, and contemporary issues, collected by Dr. Alan Godlas, a professor at the University of Georgia.

Publisher's Note: The websites listed on this page were active at the time of publication. The publisher is not responsible for websites that have changed their address or discontinued operation since the date of publication. The publisher reviews and updates the websites each time the book is reprinted.

Index

Abraham, 15, 33–34, 72
Abu Bakr, 22
Adam, 33
Afghanistan, 13, 40, 45, 66–67, 71, 85
al-Hajar al-Aswad, 33–34
Al-Haram al-Sharif, **71**
Algeria, 25, 39, 41, 66
Ali, **21**, 22, 38
bin Ali, Sharif Hussein, 75
Allah, 15–16, 19, 20, 30, 33
    See also Islam
Arab League, 78
Arafat, Yasir, 80, 81–82
arranged marriage, 44, **47**, 48
    See also marriage
art, Islamic, 31
Al-Ashaikh, Shaikh Abdulaziz, 95, 97
Azerbaijan, 22

Baghdad, Iraq, **96**
Bahrain, 22, 40, 69
Balfour, Arthur James Lord, 75
Balfour Declaration, 75
    See also Israeli-Palestinian conflict
Bangladesh, 39, 61, 69
Barak, Ehud, 81
Battle of Karbala, **21**, **22**, 38
Begin, Menachem, **79**
Bhutto, Benazir, 61
    See also women
Brunei, 39
Burkholder, Richard W., 12, 46
Bush, George W., 24, 82, 97

calendar, Islamic, 36–37, 38
Camp David Accords, 78–79
    See also Israeli-Palestinian conflict
Carter, Jimmy, 78, **79**
charity, 32, 36
    See also five pillars of Islam
Christianity, 15, 20, 22–24, 38, 48, 73
    See also Islam; Judaism

Clemenceau, Georges, **74**
Clinton, Bill, 80–82
Cold War, 78
    See also Soviet Union
crime, **12**
Crusades, 22–24
culture, Islamic, 20–21, 43–51, 55–59, 62
    See also Islam

divorce (*talaq*), 55–59
    See also marriage

education, 51, **52**, 53–55, **56**, 92
Egypt, 24, 39, 55, 62, 64, 69, 77, 78
Eid al-Adha, 38
    See also holidays
Eid al-Fitr, 37–38
    See also holidays
European colonization, 24–25

family life, 48–51
    See also culture, Islamic; marriage
fasting, 32–33, 37
    See also five pillars of Islam
female genital mutilation (FGM), 67–68
    See also women
five pillars of Islam, 30–34
    See also Islam
France, 24–25, **74**, 75
Freedom House, 39
fundamentalists, Islamic. See Islamists (Islamic fundamentalists)

Gallup Poll of the Islamic World, 10–13, **96**
    divorce, 57–58
    education, **52**, 53–55, **56**
    Israeli-Palestinian conflict, 83–85
    marriage and family life, 43, 46, **47**, **50**, 51
    Muslims' view of the West, **12**, 83–85, 87–93, **94**
government, 39–41
Great Britain, 24–25, **74**, 75–76

Index

Great Mosque (Mecca), *32*, 33
Gulf War (1991), 80

Hadith, 34–35, 57
    See *also* Qur'an; Sunna
Hamas, 80
    See *also* Israeli-Palestinian conflict
Hassan, Riffat, 68
Hassan II Mosque, *89*
henna, 45
    See *also* marriage
holidays, 32–33, 36–38
    See *also* Islam
human rights, 40, 68, 80, 92
Hussein, *21*, 22, 38
Hussein, Saddam, 72

India, 22, 25, 39, 66
Indonesia, 10, 25, 26, 39, 53, *56*, 61, 64, 69, 71, 83, 84, 91, 92
intifada, 80, 81
    See *also* Israeli-Palestinian conflict
Iran, 10–11, 22, 26, 39, 41, 51, 61–62, 66, 71, 83, 84, 91, 92
Iraq, 13, 22, 39, 65, 71–72, *74*, 75, 85, *86*, *96*
Ishmael, 33
Islam, 98–99
    calendar, 36–37, 38
    and the Crusades, 22–24
    and culture, 20–21
    division of, into sects, 21–22
    and divorce (talaq), 55–59
    five pillars of, 30–34
    founding of, 15–19
    holidays of, 32–33, 36–38
    and the Israeli-Palestinian conflict, 82–85
    law (Sharia), 38–39, 41, 57, 66, 67, 95
    and marriage and family life, 43–51, 62
    population of followers, 9–10
    spread of, 19–20
    and the United States, 24–27, 40, 41, 53, 71–72, 78–85, 87–93, 96, 97–99
    and Western values, 88–93, *96*
    and women, *35*, 36, 40, 41, 46, *47*, 53–57, 58–59, 61–69
        See *also* Christianity; Gallup Poll of the Islamic World; Judaism
Islamists (Islamic fundamentalists), 40–41
    See *also* government
Israel, 71, 72–73, 76–80, 82, *92*
Israeli-Palestinian conflict, 78–82
    Muslim views on the, 82–85
    roots of the, 71–77
    See *also* Israel; Palestine
Italy, 24, *74*

Jerusalem, 23, 24, *71*, 72, 76, 77, 81, 82
    See *also* Israeli-Palestinian conflict
Jordan, 10, 25, 39, 46, 48, 51, 53, 57–58, 65, 77–78, 80, 83, 84, 89–90, 92, 95, 97
Judaism, 15, 20, 38, 72–76
    See *also* Christianity; Islam
June 1967 War, 77, 78
    See *also* Israeli-Palestinian conflict

Kaaba, *32*, 33–34
Khadimiya Shrine, *9*
Khomeini, Ayatollah Ruhollah, 41
Kuwait, 10, 39, 46, 48, 51, 53, 55, 57, 59, 83, 91, 92, 97

bin Laden, Osama, 85, *92*, 95
    See *also* terrorism
Lebanon, 10, 22, 25, 46, 48, 51, 53, 57–59, 65, 66, 74, 75, 77–78, 83–84, 90, 91
Lloyd George, David, *74*

Malaysia, 45, 64
marriage, 43–48, 62
    See *also* culture, Islamic; divorce (*talaq*);

Numbers in **bold italic** refer to captions.

Index

family life
Mecca, 16–17, 19, 33–34, 37, 38
Medina, 17, 19, 37
Morocco, 10, 39, 51, 53, 55, 66, 69, 83, 84, *89*, 90, 92
Mossadegh, Mohammed, 26
Muhammad, 15–17, 19, 22, 30, *31*, 32–35, 37, 57, 62
    See also Islam
Muslims
    attitudes of, toward the West, *12*, 83–85, 87–93, *94*
    population, 9–10
    See also Islam

Netanyahu, Benjamin, 80–81
Newport, Frank, 87–88
Nigeria, 57, 67

Oman, 40, 69
Organization of the Islamic Conference, 67
Orlando, Signor, *74*
Oslo Accords, 81–82
    See also Israeli-Palestinian conflict
Ottoman Empire, 25, 75

Pakistan, 10, 22, 39, 51, 53, 55, 57, 61, 83, 84
Palestine, 45, 72, 73–77, 79–80, 82, 83
    See also Israeli-Palestinian conflict
Palestine Liberation Organization (PLO), 77–78, 80
    See also Israeli-Palestinian conflict
Palestinian Authority, 80–81
    See also Israeli-Palestinian conflict
Pan Arab Research Center, 10
pilgrimage (hajj), 33–34, 38
    See also five pillars of Islam
polygamy, 45–46, *47*, 48
    See also marriage
population, Muslim, 9–10
prayer, 30–31, *37*, 48–49, *98*
    See also five pillars of Islam

al-Qaeda, 40, 85, 92
    See also terrorism
Qatar, 40, 69
Qur'an, 15, *18*, 19, 20, 29, 34–36, 53, *56*, 62–64, *68*
    and polygamy, 45–46
    and *Sharia* (Islamic law), 38
    See also Hadith; Islam; Sunna

Rabin, Yitzhak, 80
Ramadan, 32–33, 37
    See also holidays
Richard the Lionhearted, 24
    See also Crusades
Roman Empire, 72–73
    See also Israeli-Palestinian conflict

Saad, Lydia, 83, 85
Sadat, Anwar, 78, *79*
Saudi Arabia, 10–11, 34, 36, 39, 40, 46, 51, 53, 55, 57, 59, *61*, 64, 66, 83, 91, 95, 97
September 11, 2001, *92*, 93, *94*, 95, 97
    See also terrorism
Sharia (Islamic law), 38–39, 41, 57, 66, 67, 95
Shia Islam, *21*, *22*, 35, 38, 41
    See also Islam
Soviet Union, 25, 78, 88
Spain, 22
Sudan, 39, 45, 67
Sukarno, Achmad, 26
Sunna, 34–36
    See also Hadith; Qur'an
Sunni Islam, 22, 35
    See also Islam
Sykes-Picot agreement, 25, 75
    See also Israeli-Palestinian conflict
Syria, 22, 39, 65, *74*, 75, 77

bin Talal, El Hassan, 95
Taliban, 13, 40, 66–67, 85
    See also Afghanistan
terrorism, *11*, 24, 40, *92*, 93–95, 97

Index

Transjordan, 75
    See also Jordan
Tunisia, 39, 45, 66
Turkey, 10, 25, 39, 41, 51, 55, 61, 64, 66, 69, 83, 91

umma (community), 17–19
United Arab Emirates, 45
United Nations, 76
United States, 53
    and the Israeli-Palestinian conflict, 71–72, 78–85
    views of, in the Muslim world, 24–27, 40, 41, 83–85, 87–93, **96**, 97–99
Urban II (Pope), 23
Uzbekistan, **43**
values. See Western values
veiling, **35**, 36, 64–67
    See also women

Wahhabism, 39
    See also Islam
Western values, 88–93
    See also United States
Wilson, Woodrow, **74**
Wolfe, Michael, 34
women, 40, 41, 61–69
    and divorce, 56–57, 58–59
    and education, 53–55
    and polygamy, 46, **47**
    and veiling, **35**, 36, 64–67
World War I, 25, **74**, 75
World War II, 25, 76, 88

Yathrib. See Medina
Yemen, 36, 45

Zionism, 74–75, 76
    See also Israeli-Palestinian conflict

Picture Credits

Page
1: Thomas Koch / Shutterstock.com
4: Thomas Koch / Shutterstock.com
8: used under license from Shutterstock, Inc.
11: used under license from Shutterstock, Inc.
12: Vvoe / Shutterstock.com
14: Werner Forman/Art Resource, NY
18: Erich Lessing/Art Resource, NY
21: Paula Bronstein/Getty Images
23: Bettmann/Corbis
26: Hulton/Archive/Getty Images
28: used under license from Shutterstock, Inc.
31: Brand X Pictures
32: used under license from Shutterstock, Inc.
35: PhotoDisc, Inc.
36: Muslianshah Masrie / Shutterstock.com
39: © OTTN Publishing
40: © OTTN Publishing
43: used under license from Shutterstock, Inc.
45: © OTTN Publishing
47: Gail Palethorpe / Shutterstock.com
48: © OTTN Publishing
51: Marco Aprile / Shutterstock.com
53: Wattana / Shutterstock.com
55: © OTTN Publishing
56: © OTTN Publishing
58: © OTTN Publishing
60: United Nations photo
63: United Nations photo
65: ChameleonsEye / Shutterstock.com
66: © OTTN Publishing
70: Arindambanerjee / Shutterstock.com
75: ChameleonsEye / Shutterstock.com
77: © OTTN Publishing
78: © OTTN Publishing
79: © OTTN Publishing
81: Volodymyr Borodin / Shutterstock.com
84: © OTTN Publishing
86: Edy Purnomo/Getty Images
89: Gail Palethorpe / Shutterstock.com
90: © OTTN Publishing
92: Elena Ermakova / Shutterstock.com
93: Emei / Shutterstock.com
94: Chokchai Suksatavonraphan / Shutterstock.com
96: © OTTN Publishing
98: A. Katz / Shutterstock.com

Contributors

Senior Consultant CAMILLE PECASTAING, PH.D., is acting director of the Middle East Studies Program at the Paul H. Nitze School of Advanced International Studies at Johns Hopkins University. A student of behavioral sciences and historical sociology, Dr. Pecastaing's research focuses on the cognitive and emotive foundations of xenophobic political cultures and ethnoreligious violence, using the Muslim world and its European and Asian peripheries as a case study. He has written on political Islam, Islamist terrorism, social change, and globalization. Pecastaing's essays have appeared in many journals, including World Affairs and Policy Review. He is the author of *Jihad in the Arabian Sea* (Hoover Institution Press, 2011).

General Editor DR. SHAMS INATI is a Professor of Islamic Studies at Villanova University. She is a specialist in Islamic philosophy and theology and has published widely in the field. Her publications include *Remarks and Admonitions, Part One: Logic* (1984), *Our Philosophy* (1987), *Ibn Sina and Mysticism* (1996), *The Second Republic of Lebanon* (1999), *The Problem of Evil: Ibn Sina's Theodicy* (2000), and *Iraq: Its History, People, and Politics* (2003). She has also written a large number of articles that have appeared in books, journals, and encyclopedias.

Dr. Inati has been the recipient of a number of awards and honors, including an Andrew Mellon Fellowship, an Endowment for the Humanities grant, a US Department of Defense grant, and a Fulbright grant. For further information about her work, see www.homepage.villanova.edu/shams.inati.

ABDUL HAKEEM TAMER studied government and foreign affairs at George Washington University in Washington, D.C. He has worked as an author, journalist, lobbyist, and fundraiser. He lives with his wife and daughter in Arlington, Virginia.